THINK YOURSELF BRITISH

h

HODDER &
STOUGHTON

Ha, ha suckers. Got you again!

Menu

Appetisers

INTRODUCTION £0.01
Tender slices of you served on a bed of harsh criticism

INTRODUCING BRAINSPACE £0.10
Tasty strips of brain with a generous helping of space

Soup of the Day

MY MISERABLE LIFE £0.20
Cream of misery, made with blood, sweat and tears

MY MISERABLE LIFE (PART 2) £0.55
Further misery, strained and blended with pity

Mains

HELP YOURSELF TO HEALTH £0.31
*Traditional diseases and offal served with blanched Old Wives Tales
and a locally sourced fried egg*

HELP YOURSELF TO SCIENCE £0.67
A blend of physics and astronomy served on a bed of crispy formulae

HELP YOURSELF TO DATING £0.75
Personal advertising served with a Valentine's puree and a side of code words

HELP YOURSELF TO ANGER MANAGEMENT £0.95
Arrrrrrrrrrrrrrrrrrrgh!!!!!!!!

HELP YOURSELF TO DEAL WITH DEBT £1.01
Crispy burnt pub, with insurance claim forms and a Darwinian gravy

HELP YOURSELF TO SUCCESS £1.17
12oz Success Quiz, with diluted goals and a generous portion of coping mechanisms

Extra egg on all dishes – 25p
A service charge of 10% will be added to all bills

Desserts

HELP YOURSELF TO FOOD
£1.41
A traditional English favourite with a British twist

MIND / BODY HARMONY
£1.86
A juicy medley of mind and body, served with chocolate sauce

HELP YOURSELF TO HAPPINESS
£1.89
Double-chocolate laughter topped with sprinkles of humour

Refreshments

DODGER ROGERS
£2.24
Light, frothy, palate-cleansing sorbet of cowardice

BREATHING TECHNIQUES
£2.30
Nothing fancy, just tea, coffee and breathing techniques

And to Finish...

HELP YOURSELF TO A BETTER DEATH
£2.33
A selection of ways to die, including assassination, on the job and on the bog

CONCLUSION
£2.53
Boiled-down wisdom in a bite-sized chunk

Extra egg on all dishes – 25p
All parties of 3 or more people must settle the bill in full

1 **Introduction**

1.1 Think Yourself British:
Britain's Best Help Yourself Book

Hello and welcome to your new life. May I be the first to say that buying this book is easily the best thing you've done all year.[1] The second best thing you can do is read it; though frankly, I've got your money now, so I win. You've Helped Me, to Help Myself.

My last book was all about helping Great Britain get back on her feet by providing an injection of **Common Sense** to make up for all the balls and waffle we've been subjected to in this once great nation of ours. This time it's personal – I'm offering to step out from behind the taps here and try to show you the way.

Let's get started: take a moment right now to consider how you yourself feel. Tired? Listless? Devoid of purpose? Drifting? Tongue like sandpaper? That's a hangover, most likely, but it could be how you feel in general as well as how you feel this morning as a result of last night. And the chances are you caned it last night because of this general feeling: you, like so many others in Broken Britain, have lost your way. Which is why I have written (well, dictated, be reasonable) this book, **THINK YOURSELF BRITISH**.

Because thinking yourself British is the key. Who knows more about keeping the backbone straight and the upper lip stiff than we British? Who is better at putting a brave face on things and repressing our real feelings than us? Who can meet with triumph and disaster and treat those two impostors just the same like we can (ie, with the help of beautiful British beer, and perhaps with more cheering when it's a triumph and more swearing and punching things when it's a disaster)? Answer: no one.

---
[1] Unless of course you've shoplifted this. Shame On You!

The sooner we can get more people thinking more British the better it will be for everyone. And I'm not talking about some Jamie Oliver-style scheme where you get your mate to eat a courgette and then tell everyone about it in the hope that the population of Rotherham will start to shop at Sainsburys. I'm talking about something that <u>actually might be some use</u>.

THINK YOURSELF BRITISH is the last Help Yourself Book you will ever need to buy[2]. (And you do have to buy it, despite what it says on the cover, you can't just help yourself). Life is a complex business, and as the world has become more and more complicated it has become harder and harder to find a way through the modern maze. The bookshelves are positively groaning with Help Yourself books of every kind, hypnotists, homeopaths, homeosexuals, they've all got their view on how best to Help Yourself[3] through today's world, so I thought I should Help Myself to a bit of the Help Yourself action.

After all, what could be more British than Helping Yourself? Just look at the news any time there's a surprise flood somewhere that's got a shopping precinct and you'll see dozens of British folk kicking in the windows of Dixons and helping themselves. It's human nature.

This Way ➡

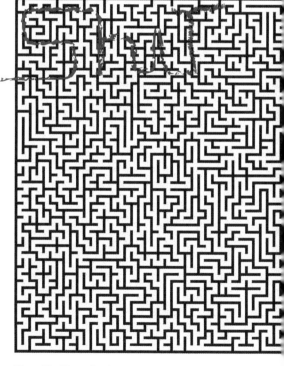

And in this life the truth is you have to Help Yourself, because no one else is going to. I have had to help myself on many occasions, and while I'm not saying I've led a tougher life than you, there's no way you've had as tough a life as me. Incidentally, the other thing the bookshelves are absolutely heaving with is books about people's miserable lives, and well, even though it's not a competition, my life has been much more miserable than yours so surely it's worth milking. Just check out the section called

Fig. 1. The Maze of Life... just give up

---

[2] Though the paperback will have loads of extra stuff in it so you'll need to buy that too.
[3] No capital gains tax on a £600,000 house **Sir John Butterfill MP (Cons)**

"My Miserable Life", and you'll see without a doubt that I win. Again. I've done my soul searching, so that you don't have to. Truth is chances are you won't find it, anyway. Turns out I sold mine that time I had to do two shifts in my brother's wine bar.

The first principle of Helping Yourself is this: in order to take one step forward, we must first take two steps backwards. Because you will only truly know that you are moving forwards if you have first seen what it's like to go backwards. Even though when you end up taking your forward step you're going to end up one step behind where you started out, on account of the two backwards steps you had to take in order to move forwards, don't think about trying to move forwards without moving backwards first, it's just not going to happen, that's not how it works. Give it up, back down. This book is designed to equip you to take those crucial backwards steps. In fact, once you have read **THINK YOURSELF BRITISH** you will undoubtedly become one of the most backwards people you know.

Helping Yourself[4] has <u>**four key stages**</u>. It's not like that Alcoholics Anonymous where you have to do twelve steps, at least three of which involve apologising for things you did when you had a perfectly legitimate excuse, ie you were pissed up. And when you do all twelve steps all you've actually achieved is giving up drinking, which means you're no longer of any use to me. Time wasters.

So Helping Yourself has four stages – yes, stages, not steps. Just four, count 'em. They are as follows:

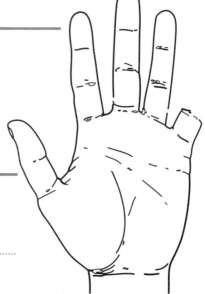

> i)   *Realising that you have a problem*
>
> ii)   *Identifying your problem*
>
> iii) *Identifying the solution*
>
> iv)   *Being arsed to do something about it*

---

[4] £18,800 un-receipted claims for food, **Nick Brown MP (Lab)**

STAGE 1 ⟹ without a doubt the hardest of the lot: all too often *realising you have a problem* means listening to those around you, taking a long hard look at your behaviour, the things you've said and done, the bruise on your thigh you can't explain, surveying the take away boxes, the torn-up betting slips, the unopened bills, the tins of tuna lying around the dog's bowl because you forgot to buy dog food, the empty Baileys bottle next to the cornflakes (it's like milk), the soiled linen and thinking: "hold on, do I have a problem?" See? Quite a stretch that one. Let's take it as read that you have a problem. You do, trust me, I know.

STAGE 2 ⟹ also the hardest stage. *Ok, you've realised you have a problem, but what the hell is it?* It could be anything really. It could even not be your fault, despite everything she said. The problem could look like the fact they banned you from driving for six months, but actually it might be the fact that you were pissed and mounted the curb four times, or it might be the fact that you got caught. Once you have identified your problem, it's time to move on to **stage 3.**

STAGE 3 ⟹ no question the hardest of all four stages. You've realised you have a problem, you have identified that problem (hopefully correctly), now it's time to identify the solution. Now with paint, that's easy, the solution is turps. Life isn't like paint, though, definitely not. Try and cure everything with turps and you'll end up in casualty (though actually it's one sure way of jumping the queue and getting seen straight away). The

solution could be
anything from getting
up half an hour
earlier, to cutting up
your credit card, to
using mouthwash,
to ensuring that
you no longer deal
in junk bonds, to
wiggling about with
the wires at the back,
to carrying on taking
the medication, to just
saying no to that fifth

Fig. 2. Please sir, can I have one more?

onion bhaji, to paying proper attention to the telemetry as you go through the chicane so you can chisel that extra half second off Felipe Massa – but the key thing is to identify what it is. I do understand that this may have been tough up to this point and you may well want to quit, but to truly Help Yourself and **THINK YOURSELF BRITISH** you need to move onto <u>stage 4</u>

STAGE 4 ⇒ the hardest of the lot. If you thought realising you had a problem was a problem, if you thought identifying it and then identifying the solution to it were tough, you wait till you have to find the gumption to be arsed to do something about it. A wise man once said the hardest step of every journey is the first (though clearly he hadn't got stuck outside Carlisle for six hours in a blizzard and found himself having to defrost the diesel in the van with a fag lighter, but I think the point he was making was a different one). My point is this: this bit's up to you, you're on your own, but maybe, just maybe, thanks to this book you can now **THINK YOURSELF BRITISH** and Help Yourself. All it will take is a few trips to the toilet[5] and the £19.99 (rrp) which you've already spent.

....

[5] Face facts, you'll be reading this on the toilet. The publishers have asked me to present this in bite sized chunks. They don't mean bite sized do they?!

1.2 Know Yourself

Before you embark on the potentially messy business of sorting your life through the process of Helping Yourself[6] it's best that you know what you're taking on. The last thing I'm going to suggest you do is carry out some kind of:

MOT For The Soul

because I'm not a donut, but what you do need before you get started is to get a proper grip on yourself. Unto thine own self be true, said Shakespeare, though the character he had say that was meant to be an idiot. But unless you know what you're like, how can you be true unto thine self?

Thing is, chances are you don't actually know what you're like. In fact you probably haven't got the faintest notion of what you're like. Of course not, you've not met yourself, you don't talk to yourself (well, if you do, you have problems that a book you picked up in Smiths just can't touch), you've not got any idea of whether you're good company or not – perhaps your mates are actually trying to shake you off – and there's no way anyone's ever been honest with you about what you're like in bed.

So, mission one, find out what you're like. You could do this by videotaping yourself and then watching it back but that's time consuming and it'll only really tell you what you look like, what you sound like, what faces your mates are pulling behind your back when they're with you, and how often you scratch your nuts (more often than you'd think). The other problem with this is watching it back will probably be excruciating – if you don't like the sound of your voice on the answerphone this will be worse by a thousand-fold. And if you do like the sound of your voice on the answerphone I don't really want you reading my book.

----

[6] £4,000, gardening costs, **Alan Duncan MP (Cons)**

The simplest way to find out what you're like is to ask your mates. Simple. But you have to do it without arousing suspicion – going around saying

"What am I like?"

could result in your being mistaken for Alan Carr and punched, and it might even make your mates suspicious. It's not a usual question if what you're used to doing is discussing the game at the weekend and in which order to do Girls Aloud (which I assume is what you talk about what with you being normal and that). Once you've got the measure of yourself the next thing to do is write down a list of what you're like. You can head the page with "What Am I Like?" if you like, but again you might run into trouble if you leave it lying around. Perhaps if you live in shared accommodation you need to write it down, memorise it, and then eat the piece of paper. That could help. But chew it, or it could come out the other end like some weird all knowing insightful turd.

Fig. 3. You first...

You could do all that, but you'd be wasting your time. In fact, I can save you all that time and effort, because I know what you're like. Oh yes. Because I know how to Help You Help Yourself, primarily because I say I do, and in these kind of books that's a good enough reason.[7] But mainly

I know what you're like

because you bought this book. You don't understand your place in the universe, you're unhealthy, you're single, you're broke, you're unsuccessful, you're hungry, you're unhappy and you're going to die. By coincidence these are precisely the things I'm going to fix.

TODAY:

Unhealthy   Hungry
Single   Unhappy
Broke   Going to die
Unsuccessful

[7] See Hardeep Singh Koli's *Law of Assertion*.

Why do you get to tell me how to sort myself out?

Shut up you and listen. First up, I'm a publican. Publicans have been at the heart of human affairs since the dawn of time. We see the lot, people at their best, people at their worst, sometimes it's the same person within the space of four drinks. There are few people who see human life as up close as those of us who toil at the beerface. In the pub you can meet a prince or a pauper, though frankly if a prince is in there it's probably a photo-op to prove he's in touch with ordinary people. I'm not blaming him, it's the kind of crap he has to do. So with the kind of at-the-pumps knowledge I have, I can, like any good Help Yourself Guru, assert confidently that I have the answers to your problems.[8]

On top of this, I have had a hell of a life. Not as bad as one of those books by someone who says their mum kept them in a cupboard and hit them with a spoon for fourteen years, while their dad looked on ineffectually, but bad enough to publish.[9] Without a proper rotten life behind you how can you possibly dish out advice? Well adjusted people who can handle life calmly and easily are the last people you should go to for advice – what you need is the insight of someone who has slashed the neighbour's tyres repeatedly in a dispute over a residents' parking space culminating in setting fire to the bastard's car (this is a purely hypothetical situation that is currently *sub judice*[10]). Only those who have truly lost control can tell you what control is, and let me tell you, I know all about control, inevitable divorce, alcoholism (though we don't call it that, we call it a drinking hobby), impotence, listlessness, melancholy,

Fig. 4. Common household spoon. If you invent a time machine go back and apply vigorously to Piers Morgan for all our sakes.

---

[8] Like I did in my last book, *The Book of British Common Sense*. Really, that should have sorted you out, but here we are, this year's book.
[9] It's worth asking the question "how on earth did you learn how to write if you were locked in a cupboard for fourteen years?".
[10] French word.

bone deep loneliness, punchiness when tired. I'm your man for that stuff, so the subjects within this book are well within my range.

So with my combination of pump-side wisdom and terrible life experience I couldn't be better qualified to be able to Help You Help Yourself.

One last thing: any good Help Yourself [11] Guru worth his ready salted is fully tuned to all your problems, and for this reason has loads of different books out at once – in this I am no exception. Throughout this book you will find references to many of my other works, often backing up the things I've said in this book, occasionally not. I advise that you buy them all immediately at full RRP so you can check out all my alternative points of view. Sometimes I might undermine you and how you feel about yourself, but don't panic, its all part of Helping Yourself. Basically, it's glorified navel gazing, but I'm happy to say where there's lint, there's brass. Let us begin on:

The path to wellness that begins with but a single step

(though we're not calling it that and you're going to have to do shit-loads more steps than that if you're going to get there).

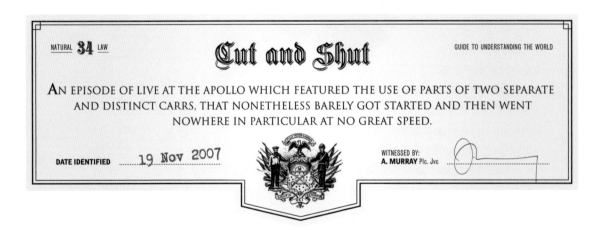

NATURAL **34** LAW

Cut and Shut

GUIDE TO UNDERSTANDING THE WORLD

AN EPISODE OF LIVE AT THE APOLLO WHICH FEATURED THE USE OF PARTS OF TWO SEPARATE AND DISTINCT CARRS, THAT NONETHELESS BARELY GOT STARTED AND THEN WENT NOWHERE IN PARTICULAR AT NO GREAT SPEED.

DATE IDENTIFIED 19 Nov 2007

WITNESSED BY:
A. MURRAY Plc. Jvc

....

[11] £573.99 television, £199 Zanussi fridge freezer, £174 "low radiation" telephone and a £399 sat nav, **Derek Conway MP (Cons)**

BRAIN SPACE ™

An exciting new money-spinning concept

BRAIN**SPACE**™

An exciting new money-spinning concept

DO YOU EVER FEEL LIKE YOUR HEAD IS JUST FULL UP?

That your brain has run out of space?

Experts assert that your brain is like a hard drive (probably). For all its countless billions of connections, there's a limit to how much it can hold.

As you use up the space in your brain, your *BRAIN***SPACE**™ if you will, your brain's pace deteriorates – rapidly!

*So – how <u>do I</u> make sure I can free up my BRAIN***SPACE**™?*

Well, I have the answer (that's why I brought it up). From many years of watching my regulars, Steve, Steve, Alan and Steve I have come to realise that the surest way to release *BRAIN***SPACE**™ is by drinking. These lads can walk into my pub tense, blocked up by the day's work, (or not in Steve's case, bad back, so he drives a forklift for cash), silent; but get a drink or two in 'em and they are able – by freeing up their *BRAIN***SPACE**™ – to hold forth on ANYTHING.

BRAIN **SPACE**™ has helped TV celebrity Vernon Kay, who says:

"I never realised my brain had so much space in it!"

Vernon Kay, Irritating Celebrity

Buzz Aldrin, Spaceman

BRAIN **SPACE**™ gets a thumbs up from astronaut Buzz Aldrin, who says:

"My brain has been to Space — I have a Spacebrain!"

Cheers guys! I owe you one!

BRAIN **SPACE**™ had a thing or two to show Steve McClaren who says:

"Thanks to BRAIN SPACE™ I realise exactly how to run the England team — too late now!"

Steve McClaren, Ex-England Coach

George W. Bush, Architect

Former US President George W. Bush swears by *BRAIN* **SPACE**™. He says:

"Never misunderestimate how hard it is to be a president. If it wasn't for keeping as much free space in my brain as possible, it would never have worked out as well as it did"

Westlife are big fans of *BRAIN* **SPACE**™. They say:

"We effectively have one brain between us, and Louis looks after it in a jar along with the feckin' money"

Westlife, enough said

BRAINSPACE™ SAVERS

These days our brains are full of clutter, nonsense and Blah Blah, and as result people find it harder and harder to think in a straightforward Common Sense British way. It's a fact that being British requires less brain effort than being from any other country — the French have heads full of recipes and erotic plaisir, the Germans can't stop thinking about the war (they're obsessed) and the Chinese have an alphabet that would stop even Steven Hawking in his tracks. If you want your brain to run more efficiently — and **THINK BRITISH** more effectively — then you need to free up valuable *BRAIN* **SPACE**™. Throughout this book you will find what I like to call, because it's my book, *BRAIN***SPACE**™ savers — explanations of stuff that means you don't have to clog up your head with garbage and can get on with filling it with normal stuff, like which one of Girls Aloud to do first etc.

If you can free up BRAIN**SPACE**™ *you'll be able to* **THINK YOURSELF BRITISH** *easily and painlessly.*

CALL NOW for your FREE Trial!

0800 BRAIN SPACE

Quote 'Brainbox' when calling to receive an special 5.2% (vol) discount

Help Yourself Techniques:

Hypno-sis-ism and Meditation

Hypno-tism is something we've all seen, whether it's someone on the TV acting like he's Elvis or the slack jawed look on the faces of the regulars when the new barmaid wears something low-cut and they will do ANYTHING she says and, judging by the number of books saying so, can be a useful tool for Helping Yourself[12].

Fig. 1. Jerky, noisy, stupid, bug-eyed hypnotising bastard

After all, Paul McKenna[13] has Helped Himself to millions with his hypno-tism stuff: "You are feeling sleepy... you are reaching for your wallet... you will buy my book... and a copy for your mum..." and good luck to him too. Kerching!

Hypno-tism started out as Mesmerism, which was named after a bloke called Mesmer, who was called that because he was particularly mesmerising.

It has been used throughout the ages, often by people with not particularly good motives. Some say that Hitler hypno-tised the German people into doing the terrible things they did. When you watch film of that jerky, noisy, stupid, bug-eyed bastard you wonder exactly how they all fell for it. There must be some sort of explanation, and maybe that's it. On the other hand, though, you have to remember that no one can be hypno-tised into something they don't want to do. Think about it...

....

[12] £987- hiring an architect for a decorating project at her second home, **Diana Johnson MP (Lab)**
[13] Paul McKenna is a top bloke and a genius and I have no quarrel with him at all.
(That should keep his lawyers off our back lads.)

Self-Hypno-sis-ism

Fig. 2. Intoxicated woman

What is interesting about hypno-tism is apparently you can do it on *yourself*. That's right, according to the experts you can hypno-tise yourself to give up smoking, lose weight, do better at work, and to not be the sort of credulous loser who would go around trying to hypno-tise yourself. The point is this: you might well solve these problems but do you really want to stagger around like some sort of self-hypno-tised non-smoking, skinny, hard-working zombie? With a vacant look on your face, mumbling: "I am under my own power..."?

No. Of course not. Wouldn't you rather hypno-tise yourself into being Elvis, or Freddie Mercury? I don't see any of those self-hypno-tised types in my pub. Maybe they hypno-tised themselves to give up drinking, the bastards...

But in case you have some other problems that need sorting out and you think self hypno-sis-ism might be the way forward – can't stop biting your fingernails/picking your nose/beating the dog when your life has gone to shit – here's how to self-hypno-tise yourself in a few easy steps:

 Talk to yourself in a low monotonous voice. Like the one you use when you're doing your Clement Freud impression, or taking the piss out of station announcements.

 Say stuff like: "Relax now, reach deep into your inner mind, my mind is but a path down which I travel to another realm of blah blah etc etc", or a mantra–thing like: "Calm down! Relax! Get a grip on yourself!" Make your own up, it doesn't matter. The main thing is it should be positive – don't start having a go at yourself, however bad your problems are.

Oh yeah, sorry, sit down first (sorry if you fell over during that last bit).

 Carry on saying that stuff to yourself over and over until you are self-hypno-tised.

 Ta da! You're self-hypno-tised!

Well no, actually, no you're not, because let's face it the chances are you'll have somehow managed to distract yourself. If you're a bloke this whole process will have taken long enough for you to reach the point where you have to tickle your nuts, in which case you will either have tickled your nuts or else become engaged in the commonplace – and usually losing – manly battle against the urge to tickle your nuts (why does the Pope look so miserable? Because he can't tickle his nuts, at least not in public, though with that big frock of his he could have a false arm on the thing and have one hand permanently tickling if he wanted, and being the Pope, he could do that and he wouldn't be wrong, but the real problem is that strict Catholic doctrine dictates that he's not supposed to have any at all) and if you're a woman you've probably had the thought of a nice frock or pair of shoes pop into your head. It can never work![14]

Meditation

The same kind of thing applies to meditation, which as well as involving the whole sorry and shameful business of sitting on a cushion, seems to be equally impossible and unlikely. What you're supposed to do, right, is sit cross-legged on the floor, and clear your mind of all thoughts. How am I supposed to manage that? Unless I actually fall asleep, when I risk the

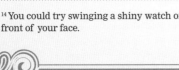

[14] You could try swinging a shiny watch on a chain in front of your face.

intrusion of that dream about the giant copper bee that chases me down the Mall and tries to pollinate the Queen's face. Whenever I try it I just can't clear my mind of the thought that I'm sitting there trying to clear my mind of all thoughts. Then before I know it I'm thinking about the thoughts I'm having about how difficult it is to clear my mind of all thoughts. And then I find myself thinking about how on earth I'm supposed to know that I've managed to clear my mind of all thoughts, if I'm not allowed to have any thoughts about whether the process of clearing my mind of all thoughts is actually completed yet. It gets me so wound up, and this is supposed to be a relaxation technique. Clear my mind of all thoughts? It's impossible!

I wish I *could* do it, really I do. It would be by far the best way of watching an England game or something. Clear your mind of all thoughts and desires, that way the disappointment pangs only really begin to bite somewhere during the second half rather than three to four minutes in[15].

Fig. 3. Well done (you lost)

To sum up: the only way I can see Self-Hypno-sis-ism being any use in the field of Helping Yourself, is if you can manage to self-hypno-tise yourself into believing it's going to work beforehand. Good luck with that. As for Meditation, I don't even believe it exists. I think the whole thing is a scam devised by unscrupulous businessmen who found they'd ordered too many scatter cushions.

---

[15] ie, the first time John Terry tries a long ball out to the wing and accidentally boots it straight into touch.

1.3 The Pub Landlord's Help Yourself Case Histories

I, the Pub Landlord, am well aware that my credentials for offering the sort of Help Yourself help that I am offering you yourself in the pages of this Help Yourself [16] book are going to be questioned. Let me assure you right away that I've looked into the past histories of other runners and riders in this field, and I've found that I am at least as well qualified to do this as most of them, and better qualified than Raj Persaud.

In case you still need convincing, however, I thought it might be appropriate for me to share with you some of the occasions when I have been able, through one-on-one interaction over the bar, to make a difference to people's lives, to ease their burdens and mine, and help someone to help themself.

The great thing is I'm not a doctor, or a psychiatrist, or a healer, or a guru (although I'm definitely looking into that, I hear good things). I'm a pub landlord, so there are no messy ethical questions to consider before revealing my patients' various foibles to you, the public. There is no doctor-patient confidentiality to worry about. There is no such thing as pub-landlord-punter confidentiality. We don't need it. We know that if some feller's wife rings up and asks if he's there we say "No", and that's as far as it goes. If it was any other way the feller - let's call him "Steve" - wouldn't keep coming in, would he?

----

[16] £7,000 in five months on furnishings, £13,000 in stamp duty and other fees, **Michael Gove MP (Cons)**

Name	**Let's call him** Gary
Age	42
Sex	Male

Subject: A Grown Man that will probably make you sick if you find him in your back garden.

Description: 42 year old male. Loves sand. Skinny fox-like looking fellow.

Problem: Well. Where do we start? The big problem was the crapping in the sand pit. Especially in the summer. I mean a little bit of fox muck, people make allowances for that. Foxes, they can get in anywhere, you just can't put up a fence they can't scramble over or dig their way under, so customers don't get all that bothered about a bit of evidence. It might put them off their ploughmans for a moment, but in the end hunger will win out. Sometimes the best way to clear the fox muck out of there is to tell the kids there's a mystery Easter egg hunt, and then everybody's happy, aren't they, as long as the kids don't eat the "eggs" or rub them into their eyes.

Fig 1. The sandpit's round behind that bush. You wouldn't want to see a pic of it.

Solution: Gary was barred. Problem solved. I don't know whether Gary is happier now because he doesn't come in any more so I haven't seen him. But the sand pit is glad to see the back of him, the dirty little bastard.

Prescription:

Signed

MY MISERABLE LIFE

AL MURRAY

My Miserable Life Part 1

It was a bright cold day in April, and the clock was striking thirteen. My father thought to himself: "I'll have to fix that bloody clock, it's a proper pain in the arse."

In front of the roaring blue gas fire in the snug bar next door, my mother had just delivered a bonny baby boy, right there on the pool table. As I emerged into the light from the overhead ~~flour floor~~ floresent tube, my little foot potted the black, thus forfitting the game. "Once a loser, always a loser" my mother used to say. It used to crop up quite a lot in conversation, actually.

Local Landlord of the year awards ceremony, 26th June
Collect suit from dry cleaners

*Landlord's crochet club monthly meeting, next tuesday make sandwiches

As I was wrapped in bar towels, sucked in my first few smoky pub breath's and howled my first cries, my mother staggered to the nearest bar stool, and the drinker's settled back down to their pint's and ploughman's. It was the day I came into the world but it was just another day ~~pint's pint's to refill, thirst's to quench, sku~~ in my father's pub - pint's to refill, thirst's to quench, scuffle's to seperate - and I wouldn't have it any other way.

Of course I have no actual recollection of the day I was born. The sort ~~of people who say they can remember being born~~ of people who say they can remember being born are liars, and frankly you shouldn't believe a single word they tell you from that moment on. You just don't remember stuff from that early, and I say thank Christ for that. No, I know how it happened because my Uncle Barrie was there, and he told me all about it. The proudest day of his life, that's what he used to call it.

Me

Ploughman's Sandwich
Competition Deadline
— Wednesday

Uncle Barrie was a friend of my father's, I think, or maybe a friend of a friend. Or maybe just a bloke who was around all the time. He and my Father would have really great banter. Uncle Barrie would always have an opinion about things. "You should put the fruit machine over by the bogs," he'd say. "Then people will notice it whenever they take a piss." And my father would say

6 eggs
bacon
sausages
milk
cheese
mushrooms

~~Start the till up, Barrie, that's~~ I wandered lonely as a cloud
~~How will we~~ that floats on high o'er vales and hills,
When all at once I saw a crowd,
A host, of golden daffodils;
Beside the lake, beneath the trees,
Fluttering and dancing in the breeze.

"Shut the hell up, Barrie, you silly sod, what the hell do you know about anything?" How we used to laugh!

It is said by the wise - who are more often wrong than not, but that's the risk they run by thinking about thing's for too long sat in a library - that the child is the father to the man. The Child is the Father to the Man (the capitals make it wiser). You'd think, wouldn't you, that the mother of the child might have something to say have a view about that. ~~First of all to have to have~~ First of all having to have sex with her own child, and then nine months later having to squeeze a full-sized grown man out of her clackers. No, the man is father to the child, I don't care how many degrees in ~~philosophy you've got in phillis~~ philosopy you've got. Man = father to child. It's common sense. thank god somone (ME!!!) has thought that one ~~through~~ through.

BACK OFF SIGMUND

My father, my Dad, was the finest publican this country has ever known. I think I can say that without fear of contradiction, because none of you knew him. He could do the

Wine Bar

Visit doctor to get
strange rash seen to.

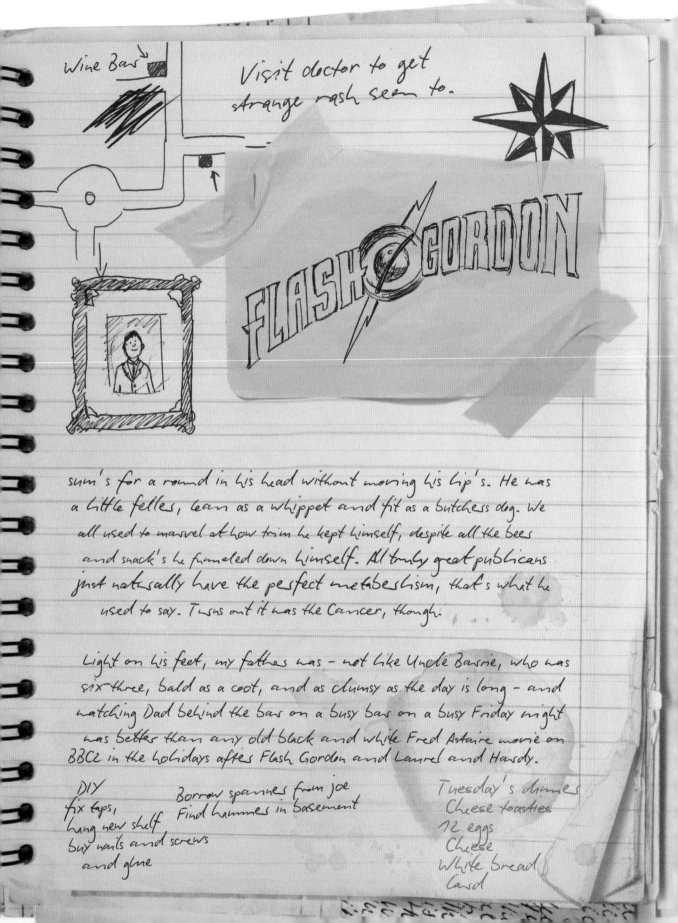

sum's for a round in his head without moving his lip's. He was
a little feller, lean as a whippet and fit as a butcher's dog. We
all used to marvel at how trim he kept himself, despite all the beer
and snack's he funneled down himself. All truly great publicans
just naturally have the perfect metabolism, that's what he
used to say. Turns out it was the Cancer, though.

Light on his feet, my father was - not like Uncle Barrie, who was
six three, bald as a coot, and as clumsy as the day is long - and
watching Dad behind the bar on a busy bar on a busy Friday night
was better than any old black and white Fred Astaire movie on
BBC2 in the holidays after Flash Gordon and Laurel and Hardy.

DIY   Borrow spanner from joe   Tuesday's dinner
fix taps,   Find hammer in basement   Cheese toasties
hang new shelf   12 eggs
buy nails and screws   Cheese
and glue   White bread
                                                       Lard

All that she wants is another baby,
All that she wants is another baby, she's gone tomorrow
~~All that she wants is another baby, yeah~~
All that she wants is another baby, yeah

My father had a gift for guessing your poison
before you'd even opened your mouth. He said it was a
combination of the eye's and the turn of someone's mouth,
like their taste buds moving in anticipation of the sweet
Relief alcohol can bring. To see him at work picking up the
emptie's after time was like ballet - not that you'd ever
have seen him in tights - darting between the tables', the
pint pot's on his fists gleaming like the most precious stones
known to man. It was all you could ever need to inspire you to
his footsteps, and take up the noble art too,
~~follow in his footsteps, and take up the noble art too.~~

The perfect marriage of man to calling, that's what it was.
"Born with a horse brass in his mouth" is what Uncle Barrie
used to say, though that image troubled me for many years
until I realised it was just a figure of speech.

I am proud to say that I am the product of
almost two generations of publicans, and the pub I
currently run is the one where my father was the resident
landlord until the day he died – and actually for a few
day's after that, as it turned out he'd persuaded one of his
regulars to bung him in the freezer with the lasagne's in case
medical science came up with a cure in the four days
between him dying and getting cremated. It's not the
original building, of course, but we'll come to that.

~~Mum hadn't~~ wanted a son. In fact she hadn't wanted a ~~kid.~~
I'm sure a psychiatrist (Bastards!!) would look at those ~~that~~
two sentences and draw all sort's of conclusions from it.
 To all shrinks I say this: ~~I do not want to have sex with my~~
    ~~mum~~ Back off, I said. I won't tell you again... In fact
no-one ever did want to, especially not my father, which
is why my arrival was seen as all the more miraculous. Dad
always thought it must have happened some time when he
was in his cups, and Uncle Barrie always used to assure
him that it was perfectly possible to have sex when drunk

and not remember a thing about it. ~~a thing about it.~~

Looking back over my shoulder
I can see that look in your eye
I never dreamed it could be over
I never wanted to say goodbye

Looking back over my shoulder
With an aching deep in my heart
I wish that we were starting over
Oh instead of drifting so far apart

~~fired for~~ ~~happy accident Mum didn't~~

However it came about it was a happy accident. Mum didn't
get up the duff so she could jump the queue for a flat, or
because she was bored, or because she was trying to hold her
marriage together, or trap my dad. She'd already done
that anyway by putting his name on the deed's to the pub,
but she loved him back then and they shared a dream
when they started out. It was a simple dream: to have a
fine bar, an exciting and ~~different pub~~ modern range
of bar snack's and a carvery with a selection of hot
meats presented on a neon hotplate behind a Perspex sneezeguard.

That's a respectable dream in my view,
and they were like anyone starting out

in the 60's, full of love and hope, and probably wearing
sandals. The 60's saw the Lager Explosion, the first theme pub, and
a new demand for decent pub grub. All sorts of breakthrough's were forged

I made it through the wilderness
Somehow I made it through
... ow how lost I was
... nd you

... incomplete
... had, I was sad and blue
... made me feel
... made me feel
... nd new

in the white heat of technology promised by Harold Wilson, changing forever the way bar snack's could be packaged. This was the dawning of the age of the dry roasted peanut, and only the darkest heart could possibly have been pessimistic about opening a pub back then.

Mum said it was she who woke up from all this and gave up dreaming first, and that Dad was just a hopeless romantic. ~~hopeless romantic.~~ She never could see that romance is all about hope, and that it is plain straight impossible to be a hopeless romantic. If you're a romantic, then you are by definition hopeful.

So with his hopeful and romantic heart set on making the place work, Dad toiled the long hour's that being a publican sends. It's a calling to be sure. We're a band of brother's, a select few, those for whom service is service itself. We're there in the good times, and their in the bad times too, and those long boring Tuesday afternoon's when nothing happens. Which, by the way, is an argument against all day opening — all the halves we sell in the afternoon to students who can't be arsed to study but would rather eke out that dribble of cider till tea time can't possibly justify the tedium and exhaustion they bring with

them - if I didn't know better I'd say it was a
fact that most Guv'nors who commit suicide do it just after
they've stopped serving lunch and the yawning chasm of
afternoon drinking looms before them, and just thinking
about it now is making me wonder if I'd fit me head in
the oven. I don't think I'm making a ludicrous claim when I
say that publicans are the backbone of Great Britain, we're
the people who cope with what the people are coping with. I
am, as my father was before me, part confessor, part
social worker, part doctor, best friend, devil's advocate,
shoulder to cry on and the most realistically optimistic
pessimist available when things in your life are at rock
bottom and you can't find your way out.

This country has two proud traditions.
Parliament, where the voice of the people
can be heard, and the pub where they can
say what they really think. Every Guv'nor is
a Prime Minister Of The Pumps, Keeper of the
National Anaesthetic, part of Great Britain's all

Living in a ~~material world~~ **important** pressure valve. If these weren't
And I am a material girl
You know ~~that~~ but ~~they~~ if they shut the pubs tomorrow, there'd
in a material world
~~be nothing~~ off licenses would be looted, restau-
And I am a material girl
would be plundered for their marked up wine,
Some boys romance, some boys slow dance
~~shops~~ would be robbed in broad daylight of their
That's all right with me
If they ~~Saturday~~ ~~don't respect it~~ the country would plunge into
Have to let them be

Some boys try and some boys lie but
I don't let them play
boys who save their pennies
~~for~~ a rainy day, cause they are

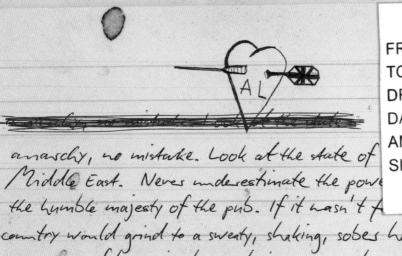

anarchy, no mistake. Look at the state of ~~the~~
Middle East. Never underestimate the power ~~of~~
the humble majesty of the pub. If it wasn't f~~or~~
country would grind to a sweaty, shaking, sober halt. Bring me
my pump of bushing brass, bring me my barrels of lager
and we will lead the world once more. The pride I feel in
my heart when I see my name above the door and know
that I am licensed to sell intoxicating liquors on these
premises, and that it was something I was born to do, is
something I will do until the day I die. If there's a pub in
the next world [not that there is a next world, that's vicar
babble] God had better makes sure my name's above the
door so me and Dad can ensure that the booze flows
smoothly for all eternity.

So my first day of life was spent where I was destined to
remain, at the bar, surrounded by the locals
sweet smell of ale and pub dog breath.

2 Help Yourself to Health

Health is one of the biggest topics on the Help Yourself bookshelf, and so should be no exception to our **THINK YOURSELF BRITISH** treatment.

The thing about the Health business, whether it's your organised medical community or the flaky bunch of self-styled "wellness" gurus, is that they're all at it. They're all on the make, trying to take advantage of you when you're at your lowest ebb.

In this day and age we're beset by Health warnings everywhere we look. If something's nice the chances are it's bad for you, and if it's not only nice but also absolutely bloody essential, especially seeing as it's been a year, they tell you it will make you blind. In my line of work I'm forever coming across warnings to "Drink Responsibly", which is really irritating. Not only does it suck all the joy out of it, but "responsibly" is far too long a word to read when you're pissed, let alone pronounce for the copper who's just pulled over your weaving Daimler Sov.

Fig. 1. Yes, but how many youngsters die smoking? Stop treating us like idiots

The point is this: Health is all a lot less complicated than it seems. That's because it's in their interest to keep us all in the dark, so they can keep bleeding us dry. Not literally, I mean, that was the old days. Money, I'm talking about.

Trust me, if you can **THINK YOURSELF BRITISH**, you can Help Yourself[17] to a healthy British body. It's easy.

2.1 Health: a brief history

In the olden days your average bloke type feller had a life expectancy of about thirty. There was shit absolutely everywhere you looked, and the water couldn't be trusted, so everybody drank beer all the time. Small beer, it was called, because it didn't have much alcohol in it, it was like that bloody pointless stuff that Lawrie McMenemy used to advertise on the telly all the time. You had to drink gallons of the stuff to get pissed up, and sure enough that's what people used to do[18]. It was a golden age for publicans.

Fig. 2. The good old days

You never used to know what was going to carry you off, but there was quite a short shortlist of things to choose from. That's once you'd dodged war, civil war, droit-de-seigneur[19], religious intolerance, broken heart, stabbing, being trampled by cattle, highwaymen (dandy or other) and rogues. There were your five basic diseases to worry about. You had your ague, your palsy, your plague, your pox, and you had your dropsy. There was also rickets or the gout, but they were rarely fatal unless they caused the sufferer to trip up and fall down a flight of stairs.

[17] Paid £8,000 too much after claiming for her full mortgage payments despite only being entitled to the interest, **Clare Short MP (Lab)**
[18] Known in the trade as The Golden Age For Publicans.
[19] French phrase, meaning rich blokes could do whatever they liked to you.

Doctors had a small group of things to try, before resorting to bedside manner and sympathy. They could drill a hole in your head to let the vapours out, they could stick leeches all over your body to suck out your blood, and they could call a priest. Everyone knew where they stood.

As the centuries passed, things gradually got cleaner and cleaner, until we reached the comparatively fragrant environment we enjoy today. People became healthier and healthier, and lived longer and longer. This was despite the invention of a couple of exciting new diseases like consumption and jaundice, which allowed doctors to add recommending a long holiday somewhere nice and warm to their list of techniques.

Doctors became frustrated because there wasn't so much for them to do any more. They came up with hitting you on the knee with a little rubber hammer, just for something to do, and invented the stethoscope so they could listen to the gurgling of the patient's breakfast going down, but it wasn't really doing it for them. They wanted more. After all, they'd been at medical school for six years, and had consequently organised six rag week pranks where they pranced around the shopping centre in stockings and suspenders, and they wanted it not to have been a complete waste of time and money.

So what did the doctors do? Well, they started inventing more diseases, that's what they did. They started with some straightforward germs, moved on to bacteria and viruses, and then someone came up with the brilliant notion of devising obscure ailments that only a few people would ever get, and naming them after themselves.

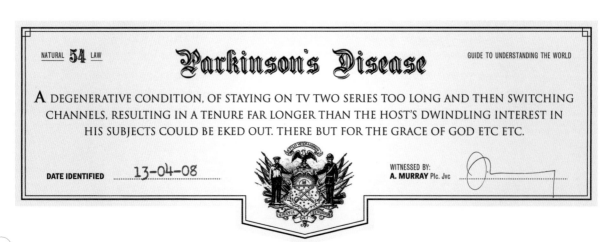

NATURAL **54** LAW

Parkinson's Disease

GUIDE TO UNDERSTANDING THE WORLD

A DEGENERATIVE CONDITION, OF STAYING ON TV TWO SERIES TOO LONG AND THEN SWITCHING CHANNELS, RESULTING IN A TENURE FAR LONGER THAN THE HOST'S DWINDLING INTEREST IN HIS SUBJECTS COULD BE EKED OUT. THERE BUT FOR THE GRACE OF GOD ETC ETC.

DATE IDENTIFIED 13-04-08

WITNESSED BY:
A. MURRAY Plc. Jvc

2.2 *Invent Your Own Disease*

Fig. 3. Parkinson's...it just lingers

It wasn't long before the doctors realised they were onto something. Dr Parkinson, Sir Michael's dad, he invented Parkinson's Disease, and once the royalties started pouring in he never had to work again. Just sat at home listening to Michael banging on about how he interviewed Muhammad Ali and Billy Connolly, and moaning about that emu, until his dad started to wish he still had a job to go to.

Dr Hodgkin, he was next with his fancy lymphoma, and pretty soon he was minted too. Dr Al Z. Heimer, he hit the jackpot with his one; he's just sat on a beach in Malibu somewhere, because every time the people who get his disease pay up they forget they've paid him and pay him again, and on and on it goes. It's a dodge.

That Dr Tourettes, he's another one, him and his fucking Syndrome – oh no, that's another one pound fifty I owe the fucker. Three quid, I mean, now, for fuck's sake. Oh, that's four fifty... calm down! Deep breath... All the swear jars in all the pubs in the world feed directly into his off-shore bank account, the fucking[20] chancer.

The bloke who invented Graves Disease even had a go at cornering the market in death itself, which even he had to admit was pushing his luck. And then he himself died of it, with delicious irony. Of course, Sir Ian Cancer[21] and Professor Gregory Coronary are the real big hitters, the real specialists in their fields. Just check the rich list next time there's one in the papers, they'll be right up there along with Bill Gates and the Russian feller who bought Chelsea, Ollie Gark.

What I've decided to do is try and elbow in on this market as soon as possible. I may not be able to retire to Malibu like Dr Heimer, but I might get a carvery out of it. The thing to do is come up with an illness that absolutely anyone can get, that way you'll really coin it. Doctors who invent women's troubles are timewasters – they're cutting out half of their potential market, and what's more it's the half that's earning. Now, if the disease can be a bit mysterious, too, so that lots of doctors can write books about it, you can get a piece of that action as well, which couldn't hurt (although the disease itself might).

Fig. 4.
Obligatory
Tourettes
cartoon

---

[20] Damn! (Shit...!)
[21] Now that he's won his long legal battle with Sir Brian Tumour.

So what are the symptoms of Murray's Malaise™?

Hair loss, unsteadiness, beer lethargy, intolerance, scratching breath, aching bollocks, night sweats and an unusual clarity of thinking.

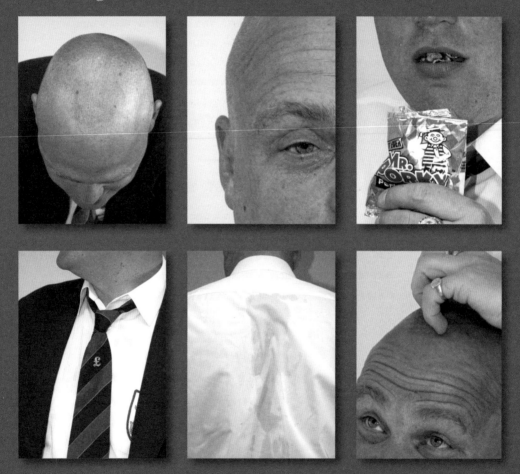

Do you exhibit any or all of these symptoms? Then please send £1.50 to me, Prof. Al Murray the Pub Landlord, c/o Hodder and Stoughton.*

And I'll be watching, don't think I won't. I've already invoiced William Hague.

I enclose a total of £ ....

payable to Prof. Al Murray (pub landlord)

OLD WIVES TALES

O ld Wives, they knew a thing or two about Health, that's why it's worth taking a look at their tales (don't read that bit out loud). After all, that's how they all got to be old. You never hear any Young Wives' Tales, do you? If you know where to look, of course, you can find Readers' Wives' tales, but they're not especially healthy. And Fishwives, they have tales. Or is that mermaids? No, Fishwives' tales are things like "Fish is Brain Food", and you can see what they're up to there. Naked self-interest, that's what. They're all at it. Anyway, here's what the old dears have to say:

LAUGHTER IS THE BEST MEDICINE

There's definitely something in this, given the number of doctors who give up medicine to go into comedy. Or maybe it's just that the hours are better. And it's a better source of income, too. After all, how many doctors do you know who can pack out the O2 two nights in a row?

A HEALTHY MIND MEANS A HEALTHY BODY

Well, maybe, but why don't you ask Stephen Hawking what he makes of that idea? And they don't say a healthy body means a healthy mind, do they, and that's because it isn't true. Just look at David Beckham, or Chris Eubanks. That Yorkshire Ripper kept himself fit, as well, didn't he?

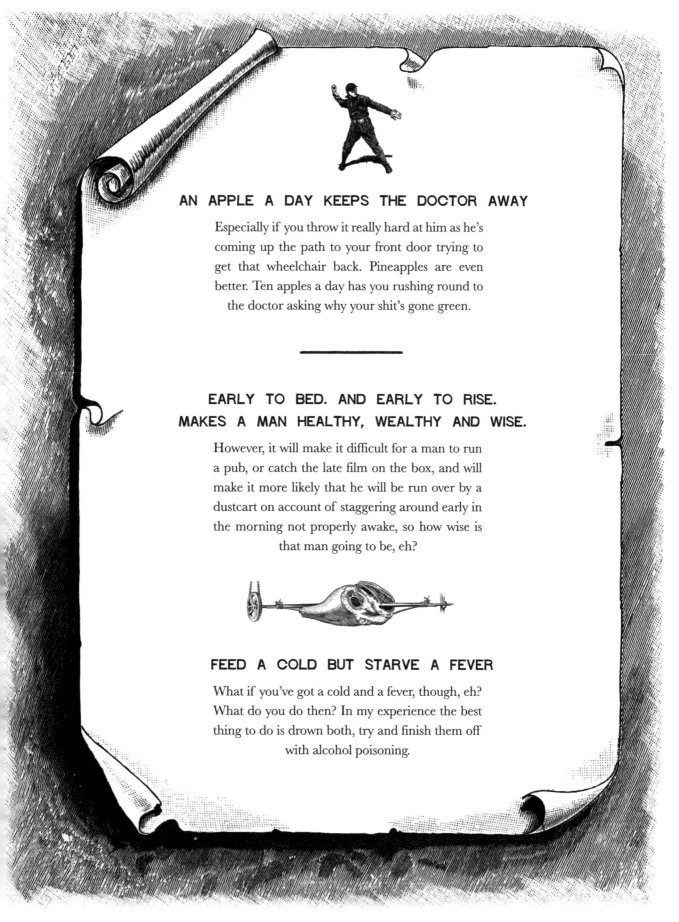

AN APPLE A DAY KEEPS THE DOCTOR AWAY

Especially if you throw it really hard at him as he's coming up the path to your front door trying to get that wheelchair back. Pineapples are even better. Ten apples a day has you rushing round to the doctor asking why your shit's gone green.

———

EARLY TO BED. AND EARLY TO RISE. MAKES A MAN HEALTHY, WEALTHY AND WISE.

However, it will make it difficult for a man to run a pub, or catch the late film on the box, and will make it more likely that he will be run over by a dustcart on account of staggering around early in the morning not properly awake, so how wise is that man going to be, eh?

FEED A COLD BUT STARVE A FEVER

What if you've got a cold and a fever, though, eh? What do you do then? In my experience the best thing to do is drown both, try and finish them off with alcohol poisoning.

2.3 *National Help Service*

The National Help Yourself[22] Service more like. They're all at it, especially the nurses, they're the worst. There's not one of them that doesn't have a bathroom cabinet stuffed with taxpayer's cotton buds. This isn't to say it's not the best National Help Service in the world, it is. But God knows what the other ones are like.

The trouble with going to the doctor's is the waiting room, with its out of date women's magazines and highly contagious small children running around all over the place. You've only gone in there because, not to put too fine a point on it, you think you've felt a lump. By the time you get out of there the doctor has told you it was only a stray pork scratching whose hair has become somehow entangled with your own, but you've caught pleurisy.

Why can't we have something like the Haynes Manual I've got for the Daimler Sov, but for the Body of the Human Bean? Then we could just fix ourselves if something went wrong, couldn't we? There'd be the odd hypo-chondriac leafing through it all day long going: "Got, got, got, had, need, got, got, got swapsies, got... etc.," but in these days of spare part surgery and cutbacks in the Help Service – it's always cutbacks, isn't it? They must have started with a right pile of money to begin with – why can't we just learn to fix ourselves, in the spirit of DIY it yourself? Every now and then you'd have to spend a few weeks up on bricks in the driveway under a tarpaulin waiting for, say, your new liver to come in stock, but surely it would be an improvement on the current system, so why can't we do it? The doctors have it all sewn up, that's why, sewn up tight like a vasectomy scar. They're all at it...

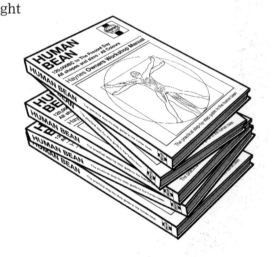

[22] Asked repeatedly to submit receipts for thousands in claims for security and cleaning at his second home, **Ken Clarke MP (Cons)**

Why the Health Experts are Wrong, a Pocket Guide

Experts say:

Red meat is bad for you. ✗

Landlord says:

Bollocks. It's green meat that's bad for you. That will really start up a war on both fronts, if you're not careful.

Experts say:

Drinking two litres of water a day is essential for your health.

Landlord says:

Surely you mean three and a half pints, don't you, not two litres? And beer, not water, for crying out loud.

Doctor's Signature

I'm not a doctor! How many times?

2.4 How the Body of the Human Bean Works

The human bean body is a finely tuned chemical engine that responds to the slightest alteration in environment, sustenance and circumstances – which is why eating dry roast nuts on a roller coaster in the rain with four pints inside you might well do your head in, or enable you to redigest your lunch.

Once you understand how the human bean body works you'll be able to make simple straightforward Help Yourself [23] decisions about how to look after it. The basic thing to remember is that you are indestructible right up to the point when things start going wrong – it's amazing what you can chuck at the human bean body and it just bounces back every time (though the older you get the longer it takes) [24].

Here are some things worth knowing about the human bean body:

Like the surface of planet earth, the human bean body is four-fifths water, though without the fish. Your skin basically keeps the water in, and it has certain exit points; if it starts to come out of places other than where it usually

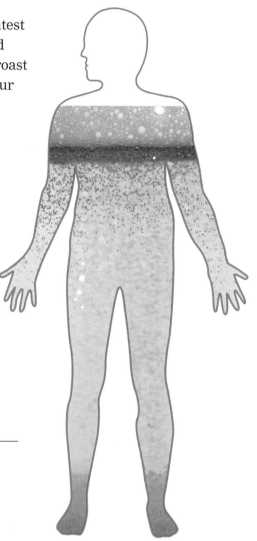

Fig. 5. An average punter

[23] £115 to replace 25 light bulbs, £2,191 for odd jobs, **David Willetts (Cons)**
[24] Before we go any further I would like to point out that I am not a Doctor, that I have no medical or fizziological qualifications of any kind, and that most of this advice is off the top of my head. If any of it is dressed up in sciencey language it's because that's what those people who plainly aren't doctors but tell you what to eat do.

BRAIN SPACE ™ *SAVER #1*

The Romans – disgusting

The Ancient Romans impressed the world with their Empire and their straight roads and underfloor heating – but it is a well known fact that they cleaned their teeth with piss. Which makes the film *Gladiator* not quite so noble.

BRAIN S P A C E ™ *saved:* **3.6%**

TOTAL BRAIN SPACE SAVED (%)

does you've probably got a problem. If the soles of your feet or your fingernails are leaking, you're in trouble. Though I don't know what with, I'm not a doctor[25].

What the body is full of, or at least the regular pub-going body is full of, is toxins. Toxins are things like the dust off dry roast peanuts, the hairs from pork scratchings, inhaled belly button lint, alcohol, old food, that kind of thing. The best way to get rid of toxins is to de-tox. The thing is though the best way to de-tox is probably what you're doing right now, sitting on the throne and having a good old clear out. That's how your body de-toxes, and that's why your poo stinks, because it's full of the nasty things your body no longer needs. Celebrities are so stupid they think the best way to de-tox is to stick a tube up their jacksie and flush out whatever's up there with a hose. This is wrong. It is rare in the modern world that you can say something with such cast iron certainty, but this is utterly totally and completely wrong, like the Euro (except when you go abroad I'm told in which case it's most convenient, not that it affects me). There is no way on God's Earth that your jacksie was designed to have a hose shoved up it etc, it's just not right, indeed it's wrong. While it's nothing like laying an egg, going to the toilet is like laying an egg, it'll come when it's ready and not before. If you tried flushing eggs out with a hose they'd come pre-scrambled. Actually I'd rather not talk about this any more.

....

[25] You were warned.

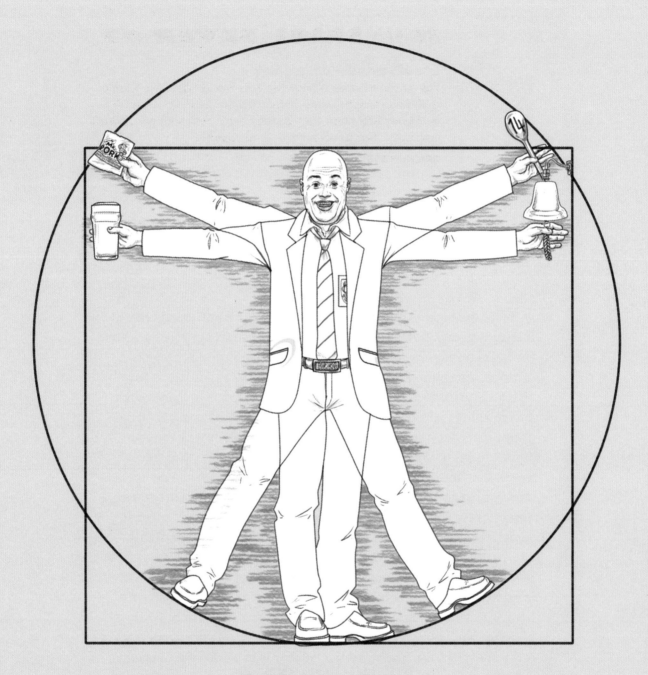

THE PERFECT HUMAN

A User's Guide

EDITED BY MR A. MURRAY

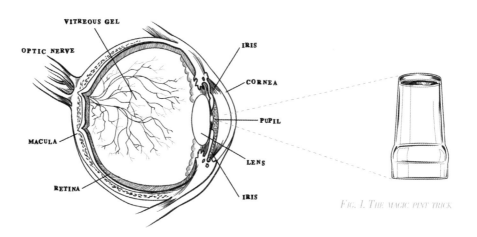

FIG. I. THE MAGIC PINT TRICK

THE EYES: As we all know, the eyes are the window to the soul. When you look into someone's eyes you can learn a great deal about them. You can tell if they're blue-eyed, or brown-eyed for instance. Or if they have just come from somewhere dark, in which case they'll be squinting. Eyes work by a system of back projection, which means in reality the world is actually upside down and your eyes compensate by turning it all the right way up. You have two eyes so you can judge exactly how close to that Audi in front you can drive – if you can see how fast he's going on his speedometer, then you're too close and he's going too slowly. As you get older your eyes change, and things get harder to see. This is fair enough – as you get older the world becomes less tolerable and comprehensible, so your body is simply protecting you from further disappointment. This is because the body is a holistic[26] chakra energy system of endocrine linked enzyme systems that work on a quantum level of biofeedback (see, easy innit?).

TROUBLESHOOTING

Watch out for: buses, glaucoma, cataracts, not being able to read the bottom line of the eye chart, not being able to see the eye chart, not being able to see yourself not seeing the eye chart, not being able to read this... in fact, who am I writing this for? Am I just wasting my time...?

....

[26] I don't know either.

THE IMMUNE SYSTEM: This comes up a lot in health books. Everyone who writes one of those books has to come up with their way of explaining it, because it is, in reality, nightmarishly complicated and way beyond normal people. So here goes. The immune system is very like the body's own security guard, in that it sits in a booth and watches CCTV all day and forgets to have a tape in the machine when something crucial happens. Well, no it's not, it's just when I'd finally got the Sov going I parked it at the cash and carry and it was pinched, joy-rided and set on fire and the useless arse-wipe security bloke didn't have a tape in the machine so I thought I'd get a dig in. Anyway: the immune system protects the body from germs, bugs and nasties, and it does this by building up a store of anti-bodies. Anti-bodies lock onto germs, bugs and nasties and kill them – your body remembers the germs, bugs and nasties it's encountered over the years and when one comes along it's familiar with it calls up the right anti-body to deal with it, a bit like the way a publican knows what a regular wants to drink. People who know nothing about medicine often crap on about their immune system being low. I, like them, have no idea what they're talking about. They probably mean they've got a bit of a cold, or a hangover, or they just want someone to listen to them and they're lonely.

TROUBLESHOOTING
Watch out for: anti-anti-bodies,
miniaturised submarines
travelling through your body,
esp with Donald Pleasance
at the controls (shifty).

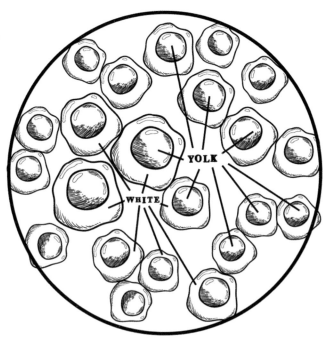

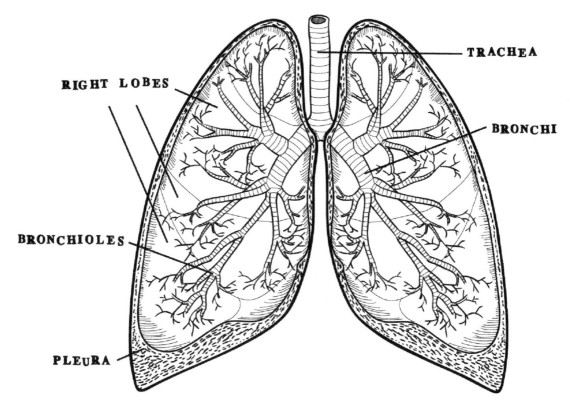

TRACHEA

RIGHT LOBES

BRONCHI

BRONCHIOLES

PLEURA

Main Lung   *Spare Lung*

THE LUNGS: Breathing is a peculiar business. What's the longest you can hold your breath for? Go on, try it now. The thing about breathing is you have to do it, in truth you can't go without it, yet you can stop yourself doing it for a little while: which is much how Steve sees his drinking.

TROUBLESHOOTING
Watch out for: emphysema, going upstairs, collapsing, asbestos factories.

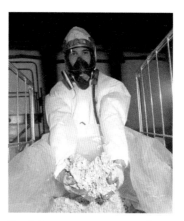

FIG. 2. ASBESTOS WORKERS: YOU CAN'T CREMATE THEM WHEN THEY'RE DEAD

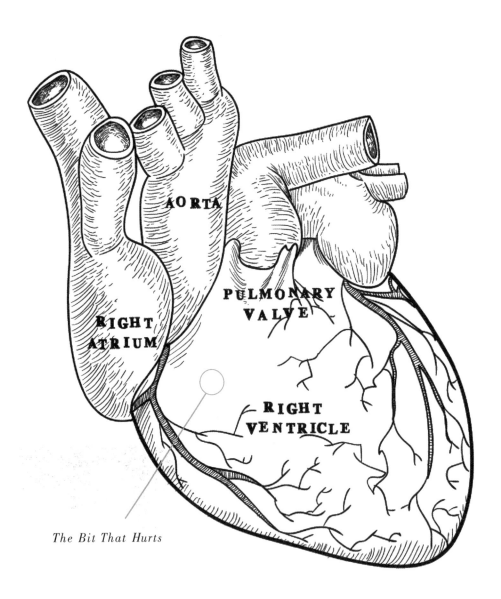

AORTA

PULMONARY
VALVE

RIGHT
ATRIUM

RIGHT
VENTRICLE

The Bit That Hurts

THE HEART: For many centuries it was believed that the heart was the seat of human emotions, where thought and reason occurred. Certainly that's what the Greeks thought and they weren't wrong about a lot of stuff like how to work out how much pastry you needed for the top of a pie, using the formula Pi. So for a long time everyone imagined that's the bit that did all the thinking etc, which is odd, cos I can tell I'm thinking in my head, can't you? Certainly that's the part that hurts when I have to do the VAT calculations, even though coughing that money up and collecting it for the VAT office and doing their work for them is heartbreaking, the bastards. The heart pumps blood around your body, and never stops, not ever, until it does stop obviously. That's impressive, isn't it? There's a school of thought that your heart has only so many heart beats and that's why you shouldn't run around or get excited cos you'll use them all up too soon – which is as good an argument against bunjee jumping as any (apart from the classic "it's stupid and pointless, grow up"). Hearts get blocked, clogged up with stuff called cholesterol, which comes mainly from fry-ups or from the recipes in the recipe section of this book[27].

TROUBLESHOOTING

Watch out for: attacks, murmurs, burn, fried eggs, commitment, Frenchmen, coldness, hardness, emptiness, breakages, growing similarity to lifeless husk, stopping.

THE LIVER: This is fuelled by beer, and filled with pipes that are hard to chew so you sometimes have to leave those parts at the side of your plate and just eat the bacon. It's really massive as well – it shrinks when you cook it, like a frozen burger. If you ask too much of your liver over the course of a life of hard drinking you may find it begins to complain, and even tries to make its way up your neck

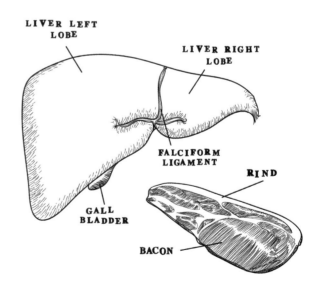

LIVER LEFT LOBE

LIVER RIGHT LOBE

FALCIFORM LIGAMENT

RIND

GALL BLADDER

BACON

[27] Life is all about choices, you make your own, but once you've eaten Omelette England there's no going back. See HELP YOURSELF TO FOOD.

to throttle you, but don't worry, nowadays they can just pop another less stroppy one in there for you and you can start all over again. I'm rather looking forward to that.

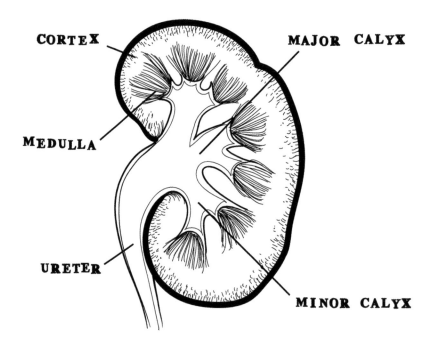

CORTEX

MAJOR CALYX

MEDULLA

URETER

MINOR CALYX

THE KIDNEYS: Responsible for producing your piss. They can also be used as currency in some parts of the world, but if you try this more than twice you may come unstuck. It's quite hard to cart a dialysis machine around with you wherever you go, and you could find you have to avoid public transport altogether. Interestingly, if you swallow a stone this is where it will end up, before trying to force itself out of your old man. Not recommended.

THE PANCREAS: The seat of bile.

THE ARSEHOLE: The body's chief exit point, and – and I cannot stress this strongly enough – is designed for use as an exit only.

THE KITBAG: Residence of the family jewellery. It's been a year, so I think it's all still in working order, but I couldn't say for absolute certain[28].

FIG. 3. AN ARSEHOLE, YESTERDAY

---

[28] Truth be told I am a little concerned that for the last year it has only had a man's touch to respond to (ie mine) and am not altogether certain of what would happen in the event of a (female) call to arms.

THE GUTS: Your digestive system, basically. You've got your stomach first of all, which is the bit that makes us look fat. Then there's your large intestines and your small intestines. The large intestines are for full-sized dinners such as roasts and curries, while your small intestines help your body to process smaller things like peanuts, Minstrels and crisps. Finally there's the rectum, which is like a holding area for the condemned turd, while it waits for the bomb bay doors to open.

TROUBLESHOOTING
Watch out for: being punched in a bar fight, tapeworms, sushi.

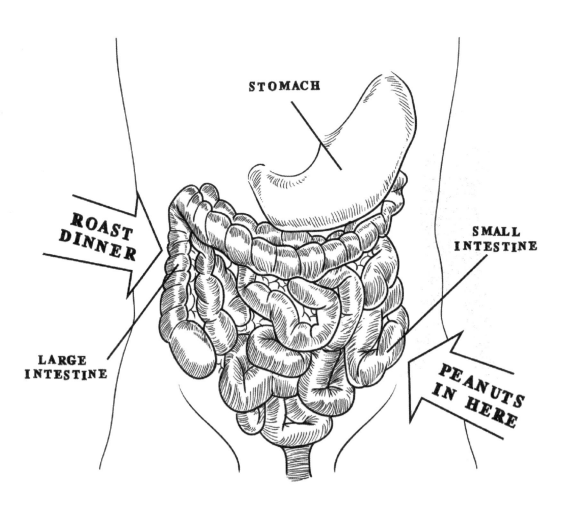

STOMACH

ROAST DINNER

SMALL INTESTINE

LARGE INTESTINE

PEANUTS IN HERE

THE BACK OR SPINE: The natural state of the back or spine is bad. If you've never had a bad back you've never had a day off work. If you've never had a day off work you've never spent an afternoon skiving in the pub. If you've never had an afternoon skiving in a pub then you're no friend of mine or my profession. Bad backs are brilliant, no one can ever possibly know if you're faking or not. A bad back will get you out of anything, anything at all, you name it. It'll even get you out of a doctor's appointment for a bad back. The human back is damaged if you don't bend your knees when lifting something heavy like a barrel, and it is this single piece of information that has led directly to the creation of the Health and Safety industry (Back Off Brussels). Thanks to homo[29] sapiens evolving its brain ahead of schedule the back isn't really built for the modern life the brain has gone and come up with. An example: slouching on a bar stool isn't what your back was made for even though your brain is telling you that it's bliss.

TROUBLESHOOTING
Watch out for: lifting, lying down, sitting, standing, walking, falling, sleeping, waving, driving, eating, shifting and shooting pains down both arms and legs.

THE BRAIN: This is, if you think about it, where we live, it's home. Everything you are, say and do is in there, in your bonce. Apparently different bits do different things; there's a bit for your personality, a bit with your memories in, a bit which tells you it's lunchtime. The brain is so complicated that no one can explain it. Not even Gary after nine pints and he can explain anything: Kennedy assassination, Bermuda Triangle, Jill Dando, Jeffrey Archer, UFO's, why mobile phones are safe, how a bee flies even though it shouldn't be able to, why it's OK to drink milk even though it comes from cows[30], whatever.

In sci-fi movies the baddy is often just a brain in a jar, and although that's disgusting in lots of ways, the only thing he's really lacking is the ability to hold a pint. Probably why he's gone evil – Hitler was teetotal – I rest my case. They should probably think about pouring some beer into the water that the brain is usually floating in from time to time. Cheer the brain up. Make it a bit less evil.

---

[29] I was never confused.
[30] See THE BRITISH BOOK OF COMMON SENSE chapter "Farming, It's Disgusting".

Zombies eat brains, though probably only to make rotting dead people who are somehow alive even more frightening, which seems like over-egging the pudding somewhat[31].

The elephant's brain is really big, but then so are elephants, so really it shouldn't be a surprise. Elephants never forget, yet don't do anything memorable either. Timewasters.

Human beings use only 10% of their brains at any one time. The other 90% lies dormant until you've had that third drink when your memory and reasoning equipment go into overdrive. This 90% contains a vast and effortless knowledge of how to coach the England side, who is looking at whose wife, which of Girls Aloud to do first, that kind of thing. If only it were possible to access this stuff when sober.

FIG. 4. WHICH ONE'S ANT? WHICH ONE'S DEC? NO ONE KNOWS

Some individuals are able to make some use of the 90% of the brain the rest of us don't use. Taxi drivers, for instance. They have to do the Knowledge, which uses up at least 10% of the brain's capacity, so they have to access some of the other 90% or they'd forget where they themselves live. This incidentally leads to other areas of their brains being rewired, so that the conversation centre is routed directly through the bullshit lobe.

The other thing to bear in mind is that as you pass through your adult life lots of things kill off brain cells, like alcohol, being hit by a pan, self-abuse, and television programmes with Ant 'n' Dec[32] in, so that it becomes harder and harder for you to remember stuff. Did I mention alcohol, as well?

Ideally what would happen is that the brain cells that get killed off would come from the 90% that you're not using, so it wouldn't affect you quite so much. They'd be like cannon fodder, going over the top in the service of your great brain nation, only to get mown down by the chattering machine guns of beer. No such luck though, you end up whittling away at the 10% as well, until ultimately you find you've only got 10% of your 10% left, which

....

[31] For puddings using eggs, see COOK YOURSELF BRITISH by Al Murray the Pub Landlord.
[32] If only because your brain burns up valuable cells on the futile task of trying to figure out which one is which.

is 1% – luckily I've still got enough of mine left to do that sum – and you will never know what your brain would have been capable of, or have enough brain left to care.

Being able to use a whole 100% sounds good, doesn't it? What would worry me, though, would be turning out like one of the Bumheads in old *Star Trek*, with the great throbbing lobes on the back of your head like twin arse cheeks, communicating by humming and hovering a couple of inches off the floor due to the sheer power of their brains. It is largely along these lines that the principles of **BRAIN SPACE**™ are founded[33].

But the main thing to remember about the brain is that men think with the right side of their brain, and women think with the wrong side of theirs.

TROUBLESHOOTING

Watch out for: damage, storms, waves, boxes, drains, teasers, training books, Russian roulette.

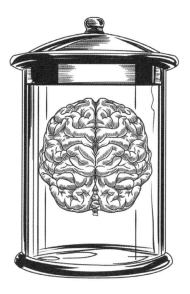

Fig. 5. Brain in a jar. Not to be confused (when drunk) with a jar of pickled onions. It could happen

---

[33] You must know what **BRAIN SPACE**™ is by now, this book's full of it.

My Miserable Life Part 2

Mum used to say I had a
face like an arse that
needed smacking. Also an
arse that needed smacking,
and breath like a horse's
arse. That was about as affectionate as she ever got.

You could argue that there is no time for affection in a busy
pub, that the hours of toil at the beer-face, the ceaseless
bustle of barrel changing and snack selecting would mean
my ~~teacher's mind was constantly on other things~~ mum's
mind was constantly on other things. But then again I'm
not sure.

You see, I'm well aware that my lack of hair has caught
people's attention. "Oi, Baldy!" they cry, "you're shit!"
And while I'm not bothered whether people like my straight
talking no-nonsense chat show or not, the fact they call me
Baldy cuts like a knife. Partly because I'M NOT COM-
PLETELY BALD, there's a sort of downy growth on my bonce,
and partly because even if I am bald it's not exactly my
fault. I was born with no hair, and no hair ever grew,
save as I say this slight downy growth, barely perceptible to
the naked eye, which arrived about two
third's of the way through puberty, just

Hope and Glory, Mother of the Free,
How shall we extol thee, who are born of thee?
Wider still, and wider, shall thy bounds be set;
God, who made thee mighty, make thee mightier yet!

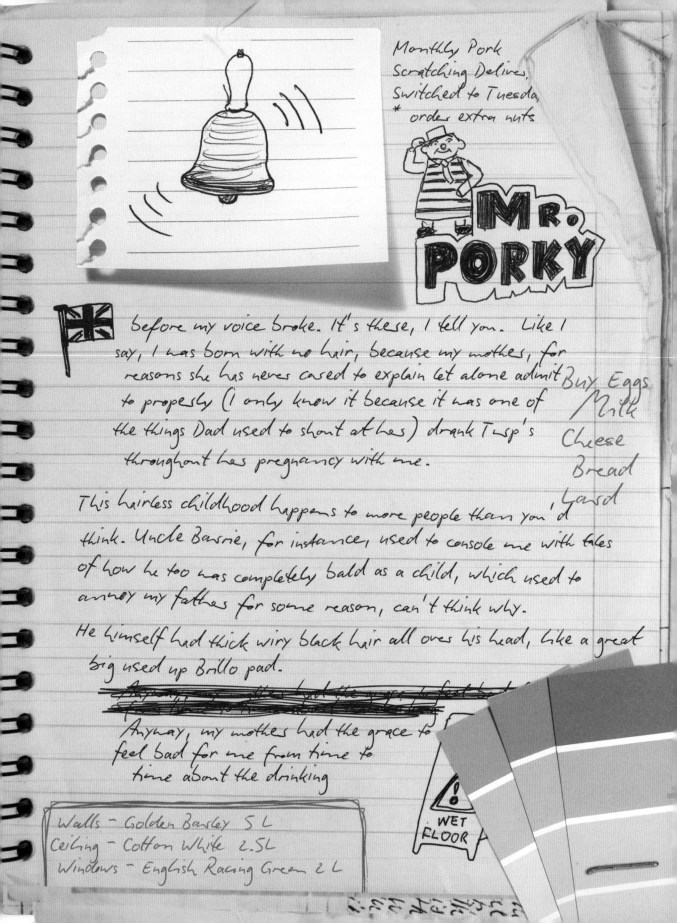

Monthly Pork
Scratching Delive,
Switched to Tuesda,
* order extra nuts

MR. PORKY

before my voice broke. It's these, I tell you. Like I say, I was born with no hair, because my mother, for reasons she has never cared to explain let alone admit to properly (I only know it because it was one of the things Dad used to shout at her) drank Tizp's throughout her pregnancy with me.

This hairless childhood happens to more people than you'd think. Uncle Barrie, for instance, used to console me with tales of how he too was completely bald as a child, which used to annoy my father for some reason, can't think why.

He himself had thick wiry black hair all over his head, like a great big used up Brillo pad.

~~Anyway, my mother had the grace to feel bad~~

Anyway, my mother had the grace to feel bad for me from time to time about the drinking

Buy Eggs
Milk
Cheese
Bread
Lard

Walls - Golden Barley 5 L
Ceiling - Cotton White 2.5L
Windows - English Racing Green 2 L

WET FLOOR

turp's throughout pregnancy thing. I remember
the morning of my first day at school she suddenly
started to worry that the other boys would tease
me, and grabbed a biro to quickly draw in a
nice full head of hair for me. I felt a lot better
then, as you can imagine. Until I got to school,
that is, and realised that she'd grabbed hold of
a blue biro.

It took till just after the half term holidays for the
blue to finally disappear completely, by which
time my first playground nickname - Blue Biro
Hair Head - was firmly established. Kids can be so
cruel. And, it has to be said, accurate.

I never got much in the way of attention from
my parents as a kid. It was always opening
time, or closing time, or just before the
mid-afternoon rush, and I'd be shooed out of
the way. Me and Ramrod would hunt for
stray Mr Porky scratchings under the tables, or go
out to the yard and chase rat's out from under the
crates of Britvic*.

* see BOOK OF BRITISH COMMON SENSE,
How to write your own Alan Bennett play

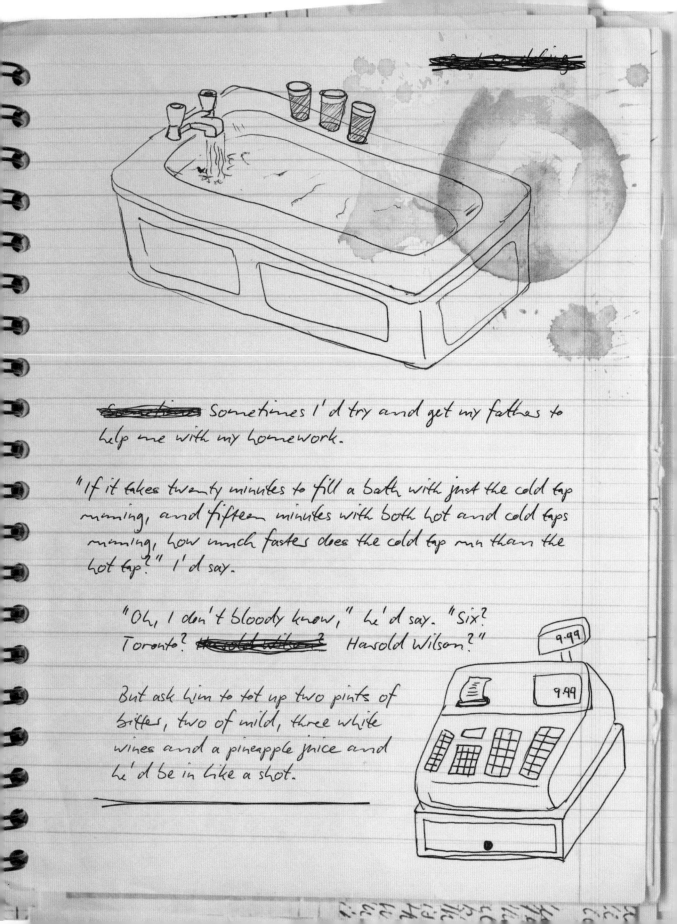

~~Sometimes~~ Sometimes I'd try and get my father to help me with my homework.

"If it takes twenty minutes to fill a bath with just the cold tap running, and fifteen minutes with both hot and cold taps running, how much faster does the cold tap run than the hot tap?" I'd say.

"Oh, I don't bloody know," he'd say. "Six? Toronto? ~~Harold Wilson?~~ Harold Wilson?"

But ask him to tot up two pints of bitter, two of mild, three white wines and a pineapple juice and he'd be in like a shot.

"One pound twelve and ninepence!" he'd cry. "See, it's four bob a pint, four bob a wine, four bob a soft drink, and then the ninepence so people think you've done a proper sum and not just charged them four bob for everything. Trick of the trade!" And then he'd wink at me, having imparted another gem of old publicanistical lore.

"But Dad? It's been decimal currency for the last seven years," I'd say.

"Not in my bloody gaff," he'd mutter. Which does go some way towards explaining why he was under ~~go some way towards explaining why he was under~~ the cosh financially for so many years.

I wonder what he'd think if he knew his son had lived long enough to charge people ~~four quid a pint~~ (it'll be a tenner one day, you mark my words...

Anyway, one Christmas Day when I was about ten, we'd just had our lunch with all the trimming's - there's no point in just having some of the trimming's, let me just make that clear. Nobody wants just some of the trimming's, they want what's coming to them. So always provide all of the trimming's.

Uncle Barrie was there. He always seemed to be there in them days, helping Mum with the washing up, helping her get things down from the loft, helping her with the lock on the bathroom door. I don't think Mum liked Uncle Barrie very much. She always seemed to be really tired by the time he left. Sometimes she'd send me out on an errand so I didn't have to put up with him, which I used to be relieved about. It wasn't like her to make sacrifice's on my behalf so I really used to appreciate that one.

Anyway, after Christmas lunch Uncle Barrie turns to me and pats me on the head. He was always patting me, ~~ruffling my head in the way someone might have~~ ruffling my head in the way someone might have ruffled my hair if I'd had any (it's not easy to ruffle a slight downy growth with any degree of confidence). And he says: "So son, erm, I mean, young man, what do you want to be when you're grown up then, eh?"

To this day I don't know why I said what I said. I looked up at my father, who had an expectant look on his face, knowing as surely as he knew anything in his life, that his son and heir had but one dream in his hairless head, that being to follow in his footstep's and become a publican, ideally the publican of the very pub in which we were then sitting.

And I said this: "I want to be a spaceman!"

Buy gravy granules

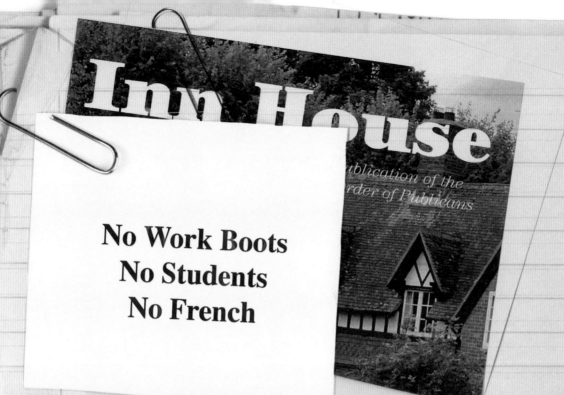

Inn House

...ublication of the
...rder of Publicans

**No Work Boots
No Students
No French**

Maybe on some level I wanted to hurt him. Or perhaps I was just dazzled by the zip-up Lycra jump-suited women on Space 1999. What happened to Moonbase Alpha, that's what I want to know? It's already ten year's behind schedule and they haven't even costed it yet. It's worse than Wembley. Or 2012. Let's face it – it's going to be a bit shit.

~~All ~~ I know is it broke my father's heart. He was never the same again. His lower lip trembled, and an unremarked brandy snap crumbled to dust between his fingers. After a minute or two he got to his feet, shrugged on his donkey jacket and went out walking. Walking, walking, walking through the night and into Boxing Day. When he came back he just opened up the gaff as though nothing had happened, but he was an empty husk inside, and we never spoke to one another again.

Pub Landlord
Monthly Book Group
Remember to read
War and Peace

The nearest my father and I came to some sort of
understanding was a few years later. I was at big school,
although I was not yet the imposing physical specimen
that I am today. I was constantly being picked on by
bullies, in the playgrounds, in the corridor's, even
down by the Pick 'n' Mix counter at Woolies (if a
sweet fell on the floor you could have it and it wasn't
nicking, that was understood). The bullies seemed
to know when I was going to skive off for a day,
and would make sure to take the day off too so they
could keep right on bullying me in their spare time.
~~These were very organised bullies~~ These were very
organised bullies.

I realised I was going to have to develop a strategy for
dealing with the bullying. How could I make them
like me? I wondered. I thought long and hard
about this. Perhaps I could win them over by telling
jokes, funny stories, trying to make them laugh, becoming
the class joker, but our class already had a joker and
the bullies kicked the shit out of the little wanker on a
daily basis. I often wonder what became of Davro...

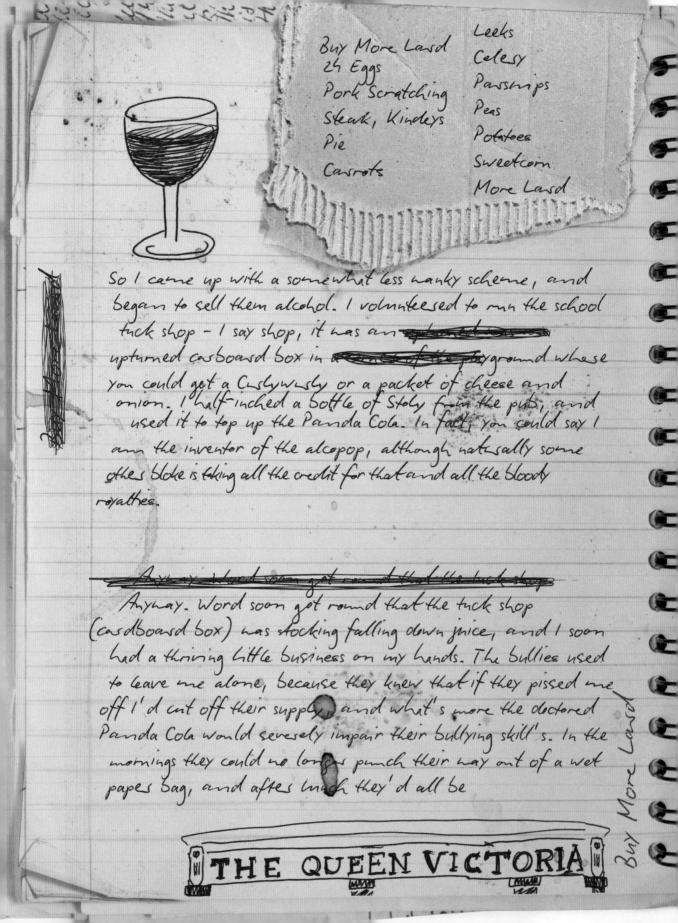

Buy More Land
24 Eggs
Pork Scratching
Steak, Kindeys
Pie
Carrots

Leeks
Celery
Parsnips
Peas
Potatoes
Sweetcorn
More Land

So I came up with a somewhat less wanky scheme, and began to sell them alcohol. I volunteered to run the school tuck shop — I say shop, it was an ~~upturned cardboard~~ upturned cardboard box in ~~a corner of the~~ playground where you could get a Curlywurly or a packet of cheese and onion. I half-inched a bottle of Stoly from the pub, and used it to top up the Panda Cola. In fact, you could say I am the inventor of the alcopop, although naturally some other bloke is taking all the credit for that and all the bloody royalties.

~~Anyway word soon got round that the little tuck shop~~

Anyway. Word soon got round that the tuck shop (cardboard box) was stocking falling down juice, and I soon had a thriving little business on my hands. The bullies used to leave me alone, because they knew that if they pissed me off I'd cut off their supply, and what's more the doctored Panda Cola would severely impair their bullying skill's. In the mornings they could no longer punch their way out of a wet paper bag, and after lunch they'd all be

THE QUEEN VICTORIA

Buy More Land

~~[struck through line]~~

nursing a right monster of a dehydration headache and
would just sit in a pile by the lockers, moaning.

It couldn't last, of course. I got busted by Mr Washburn,
the geography teacher who smelled like cheese's of the
world, and who was inexplicably fond of Panda
Cola. I got hauled straight into the headmaster's office,
they called my father, and he had to come in and
hear my wrongdoings itemised. He never looked at me,
and never chastised me, but when the headmaster
mentioned that the kids had started to call me "The
Guv'nor" I'm sure I saw a tear twinkle in the corner
of his eye.

~~My father~~ My father never told me he was proud of
~~[struck through lines]~~
me, but that day I knew that he was, and I'll never
forget that feeling. Tragically a week or two later he was
dead, carried off, as so many were in our cruel trade,
by the passive smoking. He'd reached his
allotted two score years and five, and
after he'd gone his doctor said he'd had
the lungs of a seventy year-old. A seventy
year-old pipe smoker who worked in an
underground asbestos factory.

HALF-WITS

⮜ THEY ⮞

"A problem shared is a problem halved"

Wrong, this is a lie, a problem shared is not a problem halved, whatever "They" say. A problem shared, by my reckoning, is still a problem of exactly the same magnitude, it's still the same problem and hasn't gone away in any sense whatsoever.

In fact all you've done is you've made the problem much, much bigger. Firstly, you've burdened someone else with your problem, so in that sense you've doubled it, and by the way that person won't thank you for this and will like you just that little bit less. So actually that's another problem you've got yourself that you didn't have before.

Secondly, what you've done by telling someone is you've doubled the chance of them telling someone else about it, and then that person telling two other people and so on. Before you know it, everybody knows about your rash, so not only do you still have that rash, now you're the subject of idle taunting gossip by several hundred complete strangers.

So my advice is this: keep your bloody problem to yourself.
What do "They" know?

3 Help Yourself to Science

3.1 The Big Bang

Fig. 1. Not a real photo, obviously

That's how it all started, apparently. Or so we are told by a bunch of nerd scientists who have given the whole event a sexy nickname so we think they're getting some, despite all indications to the contrary.

How could it have been a Big Bang, though? Leaving aside for a moment the Zen-like question of whether a universe-commencing-incident makes a noise if there are no ears to hear it, what about the question of whether sound, if indeed sound there was, can travel in space?

Can sound travel in a vacuum, which is what space is? After all, if we learnt one thing from the sci-fi action-horror flicks of the seventies and eighties, it was this: "in space, no one can hear you scream…" (Also learnt: "when you think it's dead, it's probably not dead".) Therefore, surely, in space, no one can hear you bang. Bigly or otherwise.

So it all probably began with a Big Flash, not such a sexy term for the bunch of nerd scientists but probably nearer the mark, actually. They wear those long white coats for a reason. A Big Silent Flash, like one of those disappointing fireworks you get which leave you thinking: "Oh. Is that all? Where did I put the bangers…?"

Then the universe expanded outwards at tremendous speed. Into what, though? Space? Well no, apparently, because space itself is part of the universe, and so before the Big Silent Flash there was no space, no nothing. Because space only exists as the distance between things, and there were no things to have space between, so there was no space. So what was there in the time before the Big Silent Flash? Well, says Stephen Hawking, if we think of Time itself as banana-shaped...

Your round, I think, Steve.

3.2 The Night Sky

It's not just the pl anets of the Solar System that are up there, of course. There's all sorts of other stuff. Stars, nebulas, galaxies, and bits that have fallen off the International Space Station.

Since time immemorial the ancients have looked into the night sky and been inspired by the shapes and patterns they see there. The Plough, for instance, which looks eerily like a plough that has been hammered into the shape of a saucepan.

The Big Dipper, which looks like a fairground ride in the shape of a plough that has been hammered into the shape of a saucepan. The Great Bear, a strangely plough-shaped creature, lurks in wait for Orion the Headless Parallelogram-shaped Hunter with his unmissable belt (three stars in a line, you can't miss it). One cheery soul looked up into the great sweep of the Heavens and cried out: "There look! It's Cancer!", which isn't something you want to be thinking about, is it, while you're lying on your back in the beer garden? I expect he had a lot on his mind, that feller.

BRAIN **SPACE**™ **SAVER #2**

The Bible – riddled with typos
**The Bible says: "In the beginning was the Word."
That's a typo, surely. In the beginning was the World.
That's what they meant to put. God botherers!**

BRAIN **SPACE**™ *saved: 4.2%*

Travellers have always used the Night Sky to guide them on their way, and when you stumble out of the snug at chucking out time it can be a great comfort to look up and see the good old British North Star twinkling away to show you the way home. It's only an absolutely foolproof system if you have gone to a pub that is to the south of your house, and also you have to be able to focus your eyes properly, which is occasionally a problem late at night, but if you hold fast to the British North Star as your guide, then at least you won't just walk around in circles, you'll be going *somewhere*.

There are many, many constellations up there, ranging from A to Z (which are two of the easiest ones to spot – they're everywhere). You will all no doubt have your favourites. My favourite ones are these:

1 **THE HEAVENLY PARTNERSHIP**.
The very essence of romance, represented in the grand cosmic scheme by the unmistakeable twin forms of the Pint For The Fella and the Glass of White Wine for the Lady.

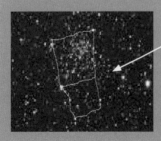

2 The ever-optimistic sight of the **GLASS HALF-FULL**. Who amongst us can despair with this dazzling beacon of hope glowing down from above?

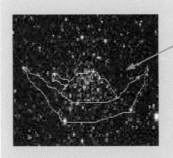

3

The traveller's friend –
HALF-PRICE CHICKEN-IN-A-BASKET.
Many a wandering wayfarer has looked
to the night sky for inspiration, and
found the strength to continue on to the
next hostelry in this heart-warming
configuration.

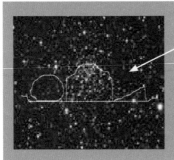

4

That trusty old favourite – **THE
PLOUGHMANS**. The ancients were
clearly able to discern a tempting platter,
featuring a slab of cheese, a pork pie,
and a crusty white slice. Or possibly a
baked potato, depending on how busy it
is in the kitchen that day.

5

The harbinger of hopelessness –
GLASS HALF-EMPTY. Who can gaze
upon this doom-laden image without
contemplating how nasty, brutish and
short is this brief span of ours upon the
Earth? Is this really all there is? Christ, I
need another pint...

6

THE PUBLICAN'S REMARK.
You will no doubt see this light-
hearted slogan, derived from the Night
Sky, on display behind the bar of your
local. Proof positive that God is both
British and has a great sense of humour.

3.3 *Save yourself some* *BRAIN* **S P A C E**™: *Physics*

Physics is the study of the properties of matter, but does it matter if you study the properties? Yes, if you want properties of matter to study[34]. See what I mean? Totally and utterly pointless. It's quite simple really, physics is something you can take or leave, and if

you don't know about it, stuff still happens, the world continues, much the same way *X Factor* carries on regardless whether you know what's <u>really</u> happening on that show or not (who wins on that show? Simon Cowell wins). So, you might not have the first clue about gravity, but that doesn't stop a bird shitting on your head does it? You might not know the blindest bit about the Doppler effect[35], but Simon Le Bon's singing is still more shrill and disgusting the closer it is, and sweeter as it passes into the distance.

The thing is, is that physics is too vague and far too meaningless to worry about. For example, just look at Newton's First Law;

"An object at rest tends to stay at rest and that an object in uniform motion tends to stay in uniform motion unless acted upon by a net external force."

Fig 2. Would this have happened any different had he studied physics?

....

[34] There's a fourth sentence you can get out of this by juggling the words property, matter and study but I couldn't be bothered to see it through. Such is the effect physics has on your general enthusiasm.
[35] The Doppler effect: in which the explanation becomes less clear the further it goes away from you, in fact no matter how well explained it can completely pass you by.

Well done Newton! What he's saying is that something won't move unless you move it, basically, I'll stay in bed until someone kicks me out of that bed (or I need a piss obviously, but then once I've done a piss I go back to bed, so essentially I haven't moved). Now old Isaac came up with two more of those beauties and unbelievably got made a Knight of the Realm for his efforts!

Fig 3. Come on. Where's my knighthood?

Well your Majesty, here's one for you: "if you spill some bastard's pint, he's going to lamp you". Which is layman's terms for every action has an equal and opposite reaction.

3.4 *Gravity*

Now gravity is of course the thing Sir (yeah yeah) Isaac is most famous for having figured out — the old much disputed apple on the head, did that or didn't it happen?

There are people who argue about that stuff their entire lives – well I don't know but the Pub Quiz questions we use on a Tuesday say it did, so it did. Good enough for me, job done. And what you need to know about gravity – so they say – is two things (they being same people who are arguing with the quiz master about the apple question, so they're probably herberts, you know if you argue twice you forfeit the round).

As I was saying the two things they say about gravity is this: it is a weak force, and it is constant. Which sounds like me going to the toilet at four every bloody morning, and is possibly a more likely explanation for where Newton got his ideas than the apple bonce interface. A weak force – what, really? Is that the same weak force that means you can't lift the car from off yourself in that ditch because gravity is weakly holding it down on top of you? The same weak force that will mean if the earth's gravity does attract a huge comet that ploughs into the planet it will wipe out all humanity, leaving the rabbits and gerbils and cows to inherit the earth? That weak force. That's the problem with physicists, they're not living in the real world (they have been students all their lives). And as for it being constant – why's it different on the moon then? Exactly. No one seems to be able to help with that one.

So, what I'm saying is: you can Help Yourself [36] *by saving valuable brain space, thought, effort and sweat by simply not worrying about any of this.*

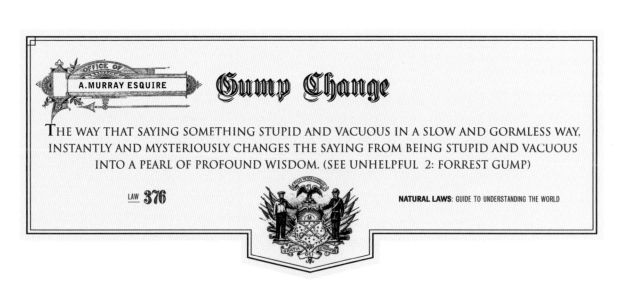

Gump Change

A.MURRAY ESQUIRE

THE WAY THAT SAYING SOMETHING STUPID AND VACUOUS IN A SLOW AND GORMLESS WAY, INSTANTLY AND MYSTERIOUSLY CHANGES THE SAYING FROM BEING STUPID AND VACUOUS INTO A PEARL OF PROFOUND WISDOM. (SEE UNHELPFUL 2: FORREST GUMP)

LAW **376**

NATURAL LAWS: GUIDE TO UNDERSTANDING THE WORLD

[36] £35,000 for a mortgage on a flat a few minutes walk from a house he already owned and then rented out, **Francis Maude MP (Cons)**

Here come the...
Fl0nsters!

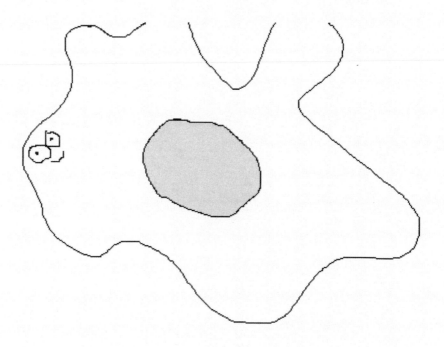

The Schniblegribworbler
Basically I was eating an egg and had run out of ideas.

4 Help Yourself To...
Cop Off With Women

Now I know you lot, you've all picked up this book and flicked straight to this page without reading the rest of it. How can you expect to get the benefit of my years of wisdom if you do that? So here's what I want you to do. Go back to the beginning and read it properly, go on. And while I'm waiting for you to do that, here's some music.

OK, done that? Right then, let's get on with it...

If any of you have any ideas how to cop off with women, write them in the space below. Then cut out the panel and send it to me. The best ideas will get tried out by me in a series of experimental forays into the field on your behalf. Help Yourself by helping me.

That's all I've got. It's been a year.

- ✂

- -

- -

AFFIX

STAMP

- -

4.1 Help Yourself... To Dating (Part One)

Oh, all right then. I'll see if I can come up with something for you. For this part, we should refer back to the behavioural model we looked at in the introduction of this book. If you've forgotten what it looked like, here it is.

i. **Realising that you have a problem**

ii. **Identifying your problem**

iii. **Identifying the solution**

iv. **Being arsed to do something about it**

So how do we apply this to Dating? Simple, let's just take it one step at a time – which is a phrase you will no doubt hear many times once you are actually dating. It's dating code for: "I am not as interested or as horny as you are".

Firstly **STEP ONE,** the realisation that you have a problem. Are you feeling restless, yet unable to get out of bed? Are you eating salad cream straight from the bottle? Have you started to look forward to *Eastenders*? You have a problem my friend.

Fig. 1. Dating - just add open sores.

STEP TWO, identifying the problem. Once you've realised you have a problem, identifying exactly what it is should be easier. It's usually that you're not getting enough. It might just be that you hate your job, but the reason you hate it is probably that there are no fit women working there. If you are a woman, of course, it might be the shortage of even vaguely presentable men that's the problem.

Now you know what it is, you can move to **STEP THREE** and identify the solution. The obvious solution to your soul-aching loneliness (I'm guessing) is to find yourself some companionship – well, either that or getting on the outside of a massive skinful[37]. Say you're going to try the companionship thing, how are you going to sort that out?

◊◊

I'm presuming here that you are not the sort of person who has lots of single friends of the opposite sex, and who is cheerfully sowing wild oats (men) or playing the field trying to snag someone rich (women). You are, after all, reading a Dating tips guide in a Help Yourself[38] book. I'm not being rude, just realistic. OK? No offence. Your options for **STEP FOUR** break down pretty much like this. (If you're a lady, just reverse the sexes through this whole bit, I don't want to keep writing everything twice).

You can ask your mates if their birds, or their sisters, or their sister's mates have any desperate single friends who might be prepared to go out on a pity date with you. Sorry, is that aiming a bit low?

You can head to a singles bar. The good thing is there is a fair chance you might get a look at some people who are even more desperate than you are. The bad news is that the odds of actually notching are only slightly better than going to a gay bar and trying to cure a lesbian.

You could enlist for one of those fortnight-long singles-only holidays in Vietnam, or somewhere like that. It's quite expensive, but the upside is that the quarry has nowhere to run, nowhere to hide, and you've got two weeks to wear them down with your charms (or other). And if you don't get lucky, it's not far to Bangkok, where one night makes a hard man humble, if you get my meaning. Actually, I'm not sure that does mean anything.

You can advertise for like-minded-but-oppositely-genitalled individuals in the sort of places where those people might look for adverts written by people a bit like you. Hmm.

---

[37] See *Helping Yourself...to a beer or two.*
[38] £125,000 for the London flat owned by his partner, **Stephen Byers MP (Lab)**

4.2 So you've decided to advertise?

Where are the places you can advertise for "companionship"[39] in this day and age?

The Interweb – this is far and away your best bet. Your ad will be seen quickly, and you will get replies straightaway, without having to wait for them to be forwarded from a PO Box. The snag is that the Interweb has so much more to offer, and potential dates could easily be lured away by pictures of Brad Pitt/Liz Hurley, or offers of a free fortnight at EuroDisney. And nudie site sample freeviews are only a click or two away...

---

[39] Don't worry, the speech marks make it mean sex.

The Lonely Hearts column
(local paper) – it's highly unlikely you're going to get any responses to this advert, be reasonable, it's a local paper and only pensioners and people looking for a cheap second hand shed read these things. If you do though, prepare for a fall, a terrible fall, expect nothing else other than one hundred percent pure disappointment, that way if you do get a result then it's a bonus.

The Lonely Hearts column *(national paper)* – stay away, these types clearly have ideas above their station and you don't need that now. You're at the bottom of the dating ladder and to put it bluntly you're nothing and the last thing you need now is an achiever on your hands.

That rather creepy column in the free papers that you mostly see as litter on the train, that has things like: "You were the sexy brunette by the door on the crowded 08.17 last Tuesday. I was the bloke with the can of Special Brew who was rubbing himself against you. Would you like to meet for cappuccino and a shag?" A really, really long shot.

Friday, June 12, 2009 **NEWS** ④

MISSED CONNECTIONS

You were the sexy brunette by the door on the crowded 08.17 last Tuesday. I was the bloke with the can of Special Brew who was rubbing himself against you. Would you like to meet for a cappuccino and a shag? no. 847483

N29 Bus Stalker I followed you home on Saturday night but you lost me when you started running and screaming. I was the large bloke in a tracksuit running behind. Fancy a shag? no. 39823

You were the sexy blond next to the brunette by the door on the crowded 08.17 last Tuesday. I was the bloke with the can of Special Brew who was rubbing himself against you and the brunette. Would you like to meet for a cappuccino and a shag? no. 847483

Saw you by the frozen peas in Tesco Walthamstow last Saturday. You were fondling them with great care. I was the bloke staring at you while holding the 48 pack of cocktail sausages and the Chicken Tikka for one. no. 847483

Saw you at the clinic on Tuesday you were looking sexy but worried. I was pretending to read Take a Break while staring at you with my legs open. Fancy and date some time? no. 847454

Saw you by the cocktail sausages in Tesco Walthamstow last Saturday. You were fondling them with great care. I was the lady staring at you while holding the large bag of frozen peas. Fancy a rendez-vous in the biscuit aisle no. 847483

ro.co.uk/crossword
o.uk/answers

In order to either place an ad or respond to one (good luck with that, those letters just vanish into the void, I'm telling you), you need to get a handle, and quickly, on the Lonely Hearts personal ad code. It's a potential minefield for both sexes. Here's what you need to know:

male for friendship and romance, to enjoy
weekends away, dinners and long walks.
Someone open to talks, trustworthy and
able to tread the waters.

Bubbly female, 5ft2, black hair, blue
eyes, medium build, likes the gym, yoga,
country walks, cosy nights in, eating out,
wltm similar guy, n/s, for friendship and
possible ltr.

Bubbly, buxom, solvent, middle-aged,
educated lady, gsoh, oha, honest, wltm
similar gentleman, 30-60, gsoh, for 1-2-1
friendship, shared holidays, nights in/out,
country drives and walks.

Bubbly, outgoing female, 21, looking for
male, possibly, outgoing, who enjoys
life... include clubbing, going
... ialising and I'm a big

Fun —————— annoying

Bubbly —————— really annoying

Chatty —————— incredibly annoying

GSOH —————— face looks like it's been
hit by a pan

Generous —————— enormous

BBW —————— unbelievably vast, may have
been the subject of a Channel 5
documentary, grateful

Sensitive ——— transvestite

Shy —————— stalker, bunny boiler

Petite —————— bulimic

Elegant ——— massive nose

---

likes theatre, cinema, the country,
seeks honest, decent man, 50-55, for
friendship, leading to commitment.
Serious replies only.

Attractive female, 50, sociable, interested
in most things in life, seeks honest,
decent man, 50-55, for friendship, leading
to commitment. Serious replies only.

Attractive, affectionate black female,
42, 5ft4, nice figure, easy-going, fun and
genuine, adventurous and spontaneous,
loves live gigs and ... kind, single,
black male, who is ... wltm a soulmate.

Attractive, calm, easy-going female, 41,
5ft7, likes reading, cinema, keeping fit,
music, big Elvis fan, wltm Elvis fan. Likes
all other music too!

Attractive, curvy, sensitive, genuine,
white female, 30, 5ft3, seeks attractive,
considerate, white male, 25-35, n/s, for
theatre and romance.

...nny, intelligent, professional
... wltm good-looking, fit,
... funny, confident man, 40s-50s,
... friendship, romance and laughter

SWF —————— strange weird female

SWM —————— sweaty wanking male

Liberated —————— just out of jail

Charming —————— after your post office book

VGL (very good looking) —— VGL (very good looking)

Plain —————— elephant man

Distinguished —————— bald (man or woman)

ND (non drinker) —————— untrustworthy

WLTM —————— would like to mate with

Gentle —————— prefers cats to men

Homely —————— prefers hoovering to men

Practical —————— man's hands

Popular —————— liar

DTE (down to earth) —————— homeless

Pleasing western aspect —— house

O.n.o —————— advertising car in wrong place by accident

Full tax and M.O.T —————— see above, or else saucy mechanic

Adventurous —————— demented

NSA (no strings attached) —————— liar

SWS (sex without strings) —————— one of your mates taking the piss out of you

Drugs aplenty available —— ineffectual undercover police officer

Now you're ready to enter the world of Dating. Bear in mind that everybody lies through their teeth in these ads, maybe not even through their own teeth (oh yeah, by the way, HOT means has own teeth, not good in bed), and perhaps a lie isn't a terrific foundation to build a relationship on, but again, you're desperate remember, so you have little choice. And the chances are you're both going to end up lying to each other sooner or later so perhaps lying right from the very start is the only truly honest thing to do. (That's a Cretin's Paradox if ever there was one.)

Now, if you thought that this part was painful, just kop a load of actually going out on a date, then you'll know what true pain is my friend. Help Yourself[40]...To Dating (Part two) is just around the corner...

[40] £66,827 on second home while renting main home for less than £100/week.council tax, **Shahid Malik MP (Lab)**

Case History #2

Name	Maybe Tony?
Age	40
Sex	Male

Subject: A bloke who was in the pub on his own on Valentine's. He did tell me his name. It might have been Tony[41].

Description: 40-year-old male. Quite fat. Not much hair, in a sort of tufty horseshoe shape.

Problem: Tony's[42] problem was one of self-image. He kept looking at an image of himself in the mirror behind the optics, and he didn't like what he saw. He felt this was holding him back in his pursuit of women, and he was right, actually, because it wasn't just that he was fat and bald(ing), he also had a sort of piggy face, and a hairy blob on one side of his nose which might have been a wart but looked too big to be a wart. Certainly compared to warts I've seen on other people. And some of the other warts on this bloke. Anyway he was single - obviously - and getting himself in a right state because he hadn't got a date for Valentine's, the most romantic night of the year, which has broken stronger men. A few lovey-dovey couples were in the pub that night, having a quick half before nipping over to Pizza Hut for all-you-can-eat salad bar (cheapskates, the lot of 'em), and that was only making things worse for Tony[43]. I took pity on this poor unfortunate, and gave him the benefit of mine 'umble expertise.

Solution: Six pints of lager, six whisky chasers, two snakebites and half a pint of Baileys. He'd forgotten it was Valentine's long before closing time.

Prescription:

[41] I think it was Tony.
[42] I think it was Tony.
[43] I think it was Tony.

Signed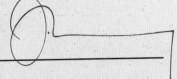

MORON

～ SIGMUND FREUD ～

"Love and work... work and love,
that's all there is"

In many ways, Freud is the Godfather of the *Help Yourself* industry, and having to study his ideas about blokes wanting to sleep with their mothers has put more therapists into therapy than any other single factor. He's selling you a pup with this one, though.

Take for example the bloke who is single and unemployed, sitting at home watching Jeremy Kyle and crying into his Cup-a-Soup, he has neither Love nor Work. He has, however, got a Cup-a-Soup. But if Freud had suggested that: "Love and Work and Cup-a-Soup... Cup-a-Soup, Work and Love, that's all there is," do you think they'd still have paid him the big bucks? Because I don't.

Or what about the bloke on a stag weekend in Malmo with a bunch of mates? He's not at work, and there's no chance of finding love on a stag weekend, not unless you pay for it, or hook up with a hen party that matches your stag party exactly hen-for-stag, and which is even more pissed up than you lot are, and what are the odds of that happening? But just ask him if he had a good time when he gets back and you'll never shut him up, or stop him showing you the photos of his mate with a condom on his head.

So, sorry Sigmund, we will have to look elsewhere for expert assistance.

4.3 Help Yourself...To Dating (Part two)

So someone has fallen for your pack of lies – I mean, responded to your personal ad – and you are ready to go out on a date. Brave man.

At this point it is important to be absolutely clear about why you want to take this next step. Why do you want to date? What's the reason? Perhaps it's to gain a feeling of self-worth, to feel validated by being chosen by another. Is it to satisfy the natural instinct of man to be with woman, or of woman to be with man[44]? Maybe you see it as the first step on the long, long road to the ultimate human goal, to create new life out of the union of mind and body with a soulmate, in spiritual and physical harmony, in order that there will be someone to pay for your dinners when you are old. Or are you just bored, because Saturday night telly has really gone downhill, and if you hear another one of Bruce Forsyth's joke-shaped sentences you are definitely going to kill yourself, so you figured dating might be a good way to at least get out of the house, seeing as the local is closed for refurbishment for a month?

BRAIN SPACE™ SAVER #3

Sex thoughts
Newspapers say that scientists assert that men think about sex every ten minutes. Free up your BRAIN SPACE™ to do that difficult tax return by having sex just before you sit down to fill it in. I'm dreading doing mine, it's nearly been a year.

BRAIN SPACE™ saved: 8.2%

TOTAL BRAIN SPACE SAVED (%)

You may be surprised to learn that the last of these options has the greatest chance of success. The trick is to go in to it wanting and expecting as little as possible, that way, you won't be disappointed[45]. So my advice, see it as just something marginally better than heating up a tin of soup in front of *You've Been Framed*[46].

---

[44] And man with man and woman with woman bla bla bla. I've got to put that in otherwise the lads down the sexual relations office will have my guts for garters.
[45] See also *Help Yourself to Success*.
[46] Which is much improved since that Harry Hill took over. And the added bonus is you don't have to look at him while you're watching it. Moves about too much for my liking.

Good, so now you've got yourself the correct attitude, let's crack on.

Other Help Yourself[47] guides to this area of human existence will tell you that the golden rule, when meeting someone for the first time, is this: **BE YOURSELF**.

I put it to you that this is a terrible idea. The reason why you have no one, and are having to put yourself through this agony in the first place, is that nobody is interested in you yourself, there is something in some way flawed, inadequate, or downright repellent about the person that you are, so my advice to you is this: **BE SOMEBODY ELSE**.

Everybody lies. She will almost certainly be lying to you every time she opens her mouth, so why shouldn't you have a chequered and interesting past? Things which tend to play well include: a first marriage which ended tragically which you don't like to talk about, fictitious friendships with famous people (especially astronauts), great hardships borne nobly, foreign charity work (preferably somewhere hot and dangerous, and not a Saturday job in the Barnardos shop in Newport), and not having long to live.

---

[47] £199 pouffe, £370 armchair, £899 sofa, £29.99 for a "black glitter toilet seat", **John Reid MP (Lab)**

Next make sure you have some lines prepared. I can suggest a couple, but you should think of your own too. After all, I'm out there too and I don't want you cramping my style by nicking my best stuff. I'd go with these old standbys:

"I've never done anything like this before but your letter was so intriguing."

"I like your hair."

"What sort of things do you like? I like those things too."

You should be ready to wing it a bit, for example if she has really spectacularly horrible hair and you just can't bring yourself to say it. And do listen carefully to the things she likes, just in case it's not appropriate for you to like them too[48].

....

[48] Maybe she likes two men at once, for example.

4.4 *Dating code crib sheet*

The date is a foreign land, and they speak a
different language there. It sounds like our
language, but familiar-sounding phrases have very
different meanings. Here are some to watch out for.

👍 Are you (your name here)?
👎 *Your ad led me to expect
someone more human looking.*

👍 It's a lovely restaurant.
👎 *I will come here another time
with someone better.*

👍 I hear the food's really
good here.
👎 *I'm going to order the most
expensive thing so as not to
waste the whole evening.*

👍 You look great.
👎 *You seem needy.*

👍 You're bloody brilliant.
👎 *I've just spotted your teeth!*

👍 I feel like I know you.
👎 *I think I recognise you
from Crimewatch.*

👍 Just a glass of mineral water
for me, please.
👎 *I want a fighting chance of
tasting the rohypnol.*

👍 It's not a date, really, is it, more
of a get-to-know-you thingy.
👎 *I really don't want it to be a date.*

👍 Let's just take it one step at a time.
👎 *Your desperation frightens me.*

👍 I'm not looking for commitment
right now.
👎 *You smell funny.*

👍 It's not you, it's me.
👎 *It's you.*

👍 I've got an early start in
the morning.
👎 *I called a mini-cab when I went to
the toilet just now.*

👍 Let's just play it by ear, shall we?
👎 *I'm changing my mobile phone
number first thing tomorrow.*

👍 We're going halvesies, aren't we?
👎 *You are paying.*

👍 Good night.
👎 *Goodbye for ever.*

4.5 Have an Exit Strategy

It's possible that the date won't go the distance. In fact, it's possible that she'll take one look at you at the very start of the evening and pretend to be waiting for someone else. To be honest, last time out I never actually got further than mentioning to the lady that I'd never been on a 'date' before, and she went to the toilet and never came back. She must have gone out of the window into the car park. You have to admire that, don't you, in a way?

So what to do when the crushing feeling sinks in that it's all gone tits up, and not the way you were hoping the tits would go? The most important thing for your self esteem is to leave with some dignity intact. The best way I find is to pretend to take a call from them on your mobile and loudly say: "What's that, love? You've had an accident and you've had to go home to change?" This way, the focus is taken away from you and pointed firmly at the other person. You can now down the pint you've been nursing and leave with your head held high, knowing you've done the right thing... you've Helped Yourself[49].

4.6 Help Yourself to A Good Night In (aka Plan B)

OK, so the dating didn't work out – I'm good but I'm not a bloody miracle worker, be reasonable – and as a result you're stuck indoors on your ownsome whining to yourself: "I don't need anyone anyway, I'm an individual, I'm a free man".

Well then, here's a perfect way for you express your individuality, it's...

---

[49] £30,000 Gardening Costs (including £1,645 Duck Island for a pond), **Sir Peter Viggers MP (Cons)**

the
Prisoner
Drinking Game

T his game is based on the seminal sixties series The Prisoner,
starring the angriest actor all of time – Patrick McGoohan.

You've seen it, you have, it's one of those shows you have seen and the minute it
comes on you go: "Oh yeah, I know this, some of it's good, some of it's bonkers".
In keeping with the themes of the show you will not have a name by the time this
game ends, as no one will be able to remember it, including you. You will, however, be able to be identified as a number, either because someone will remember
the number of beers you got through or someone else has remembered the
number of the local taxi firm to get you home and keeps saying it whilst you try
and drunkenly prod it into your mobile.

Take a drink every time you don't understand what the hell is going on (this might be enough to take you out in the first episode, but if you're still going, read on).

Take a drink every time you hear a piece of incidental music that either you can't quite put your finger on but you think might be based on a nursery rhyme, or is anyway far too dramatical for the scene in question. If you think both of these thoughts, take two swigs.

Down your pint if there's a scene with Rover (the huge white blow-up testicle that knocks around The Village suffocating potential escapees). Also roar like a wild animal.

Take a drink every time Patrick McGoohan storms around his flat claustrophobically clicking his fingers mumbling to himself in a way which appears far too dramatical for the scene in question.

Down whatever comes to hand when you can see two of Patrick McGoohan, either you're watching the episode where there are actually two of him or you've simply had too much to drink already and you can see two of him of him, in which case you've already been playing the game long enough.

Down your pint every time anyone says: 'Being seeing you.' Don't worry, this only lasts up about to episode number five of the seventeen as they employed new writers that had totally forgotten any of the catchphrases from the first few episodes.

Take a drink every time you spot the transition in the exterior scenes between the shots filmed on location and the shots clearly filmed in an over-lit studio which looks nothing like the outside world you've ever encountered but which are nevertheless pretending to be outdoors even though they are indoors. Similarly whenever it's supposed to be the night-time but is obviously broad daylight.

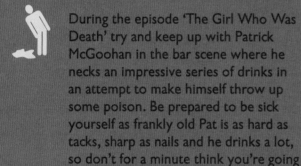

During the episode 'The Girl Who Was Death' try and keep up with Patrick McGoohan in the bar scene where he necks an impressive series of drinks in an attempt to make himself throw up some poison. Be prepared to be sick yourself as frankly old Pat is as hard as tacks, sharp as nails and he drinks a lot, so don't for a minute think you're going to out-drink the McGoo.

Take a drink every time Patrick McGoohan is played by a stunt double (a hint, these are normally the shots involving the back of his head or when he's inexplicably on a rollercoaster dressed up as Sherlock Holmes). He's actually not in two of the episodes at all – he was on his holidays.

Take a drink every time you think to yourself that you'd love to be ensconced in The Village as there seems to be none of the following there: knife culture, Stephen Fry, teenage pregnancies, *Eastenders*, Welsh people shouting "Oysters" at you, credit crunch, adverts for cheaper car insurance or E-coli.

Go round and down every last drop of alcohol left in the house (including wife's/girlfriend's perfume and stuff you've found in the garage) if you stop the DVD to go for a piss or something, and the telly comes on, and it's showing one of the episodes of *Columbo* with McGoohan in. Then sit down and watch that instead.

When you realise a) They should have never tried to even bother remaking this mental yet fantastic piece of television, and b) ITV will never take a chance on anything like this again as they've realised that all they are really comfortable with is making implausibly bad remakes of shit game shows that were shit anyway but now with the added bonus of no-mark celebrities that no one cares about, then go ahead and drown your sorrows.

Information. We want information. Or something more to drink.

By now if you still want information, and are still capable of processing it, then turn over to BBC4 and watch re-runs of *Railway Walks* with Julia Bradbury; this may not quell your appetite for anything factual, but it will make you realise the only reason you would ever want to walk along an abandoned railway siding is to be alone with or bump into Julia Bradbury. Choo Choo.

5 | **Help Yourself To Anger Management**

Like me, Anger is hugely misunderstood, and that's because the people who are supposed to know all about it are charlatans and completely nuts themselves.
It makes me so mad...

Anger is a huge part of modern life. It's a huge part of mine, anyway, and consequently far too important to leave to people like Susan Dunn, the world-famous[50] life coach, who believes: "Anger, in its rawest form, comes from the primitive or reptilian brain." I'm sorry, but am I the only one who thinks she sounds like David Icke?

Then there's the British Association of Anger Management, who are apparently the experts on the subject. This is the name they've chosen for themselves, and they like to shorten it to *BAAM*, which is the sound of an innocent bystander being punched in the face for trying to break up a perfectly legitimate fight between man and wife. That's how I remember it, anyway. And these are the ones who are supposed to be able to manage their Anger. They might as well call themselves *THUMP* or *FIST.* They should have a name like the Colchester[51] Association for Life Management – *CALM.* Something like that.

---

[50] Okay one tiny piece of sarcasm in a fifty thousand word book is not bad. Give me a break.
[51] Could just as well be Carlisle, or Chester. It would still work. I don't know where their head office is. Stop getting at me.

HELP YOURSELF TO ANGER MANAGEMENT

They just haven't thought it through. How do you think angry people feel if a letter arrives with BAAM on the top of it. Wound up, that's how!

There are many myths and taboos surrounding Anger, the Angry and Anger Management. Hopefully this section will clear things up for you.

5.1 What is anger and how do you spot it?

Oh come on, you know what Anger is, surely to God?!
Don't get me started...

Anger is detectable to all five of the senses. For example: it **LOOKS** like Alan Carr getting another series of anything, it **SOUNDS** like your apparently deaf neighbours' shit record collection, and it **SMELLS** like someone selfishly blowing off right next to you on a overcrowded bus. If you've ever seen a close up of a football fan when his team have been denied a penalty, you'll see his purple face distorted by the **TASTE** of bile. And as for **TOUCH**, well, it's what the face of that bloke who's been looking at your pint feels like bouncing off your fist.

Men are by their nature angrier than women. That's a fact, according to scientists. Scientists! What do they know? Anyway, the reason men are by their nature angrier than women is that men have to live with women. Simple as that.

5.2 There is no cure

Anger, we hear, cannot be cured. It's only ever transferable. There will always be a certain amount of anger in the world, and what happens is, it gets passed around from person to person. This is where Anger Management[52] comes in. Now Anger Management doesn't actually get rid of it, otherwise it would be called Anger Destruction, or something cool and furious like Anger Obliteration. It's not, though. That would be too much to hope for.

---

[52] When someone suggested I should look into anger management, I thanked them for the compliment thinking they were suggesting a career change. I then realised it was an insult and smacked them.

See what happens is you and go to an Anger Management class and see an Anger Manager, and he tells you first of all that no, you can't leave before the full hour is up because of the terms of the court order. Then he starts going on about how it's your Dad's fault that you're angry as he deprived you of love

Fig 1. New concept for BAAM logo?

as a child. Well, if that doesn't make you mad I don't know what will. So now you go and tell your Dad that it's all his fault, and this really winds him up and before you know it your anger is transferred to him. So in turn, he then goes into a shop and has a go at the person behind the counter and so on, the Anger Transforigamation™ continues. But wait a minute! You still have all your anger, you haven't transferred it to your Dad, it's just that now he's got it as well. There's twice as much bloody anger as there was in the first place! It's just a Job Creation scheme, the whole racket, and who's paying for it? Muggins, that's who...!

5.3 *A World Without Anger*

What if all the Anger in the world was completely managed? That's the dream, presumably, of these Anger Managers, a world in which nobody got pissed off about anything, or if they did that it was so successfully suppressed that we never saw any external signs of it, it just corroded away at our insides until half the population dropped dead of burst blood vessels[53].

No Anger? Life would be like the *Antiques Roadshow*, wouldn't it? And let's face it, that show would be much better off for seeing a pensioner lose their rag every now and then, and beat Mike Aspel over the head because their vase they thought was worth a mint is actually from British Home Stores. Age Rage – I'll be dealing with that in another book some time. Depending on how this one goes.

Wealth

....

[53] The male half.

The Co

Anger's not all bad, though, I don't reckon. It's the proper way for you to face and come to terms with the vast gaping hole in your existence. Forget depression, Buddhism or anxiety, Anger's easily the best one to have. Anger gets results. You could for example go into the demolition business, or become a loan shark or even a professional wrestler. Or some kind of hitman.

I mean, what's actually wrong with Anger? Say, for example, you punch a wall. You're only hurting yourself, aren't you? Unless of course you're renting, and then you're going to lose some of your deposit unless you're really handy with old newspaper, Polyfilla and paint. So stop trying to Manage me. It's very important we treat Angry people in the correct way. Don't send Angry people to prison, that's just going to make them cross. Anger doesn't need to be managed away, that's a waste of useful raw energy. It should be channelled, then it can become a force for good. Why not stick angry blokes in Afghanistan with a huge rocket launcher and tell them: "That bloke over there said your mum was really fat". Job done. The war would have been over in days if we'd have done that. Instead they're all banged up getting even more livid at the shit food they're being served, and the fact they have to share their cell with their own faeces in a lidless bucket and Big Barry the Sidwell Strangler[54].

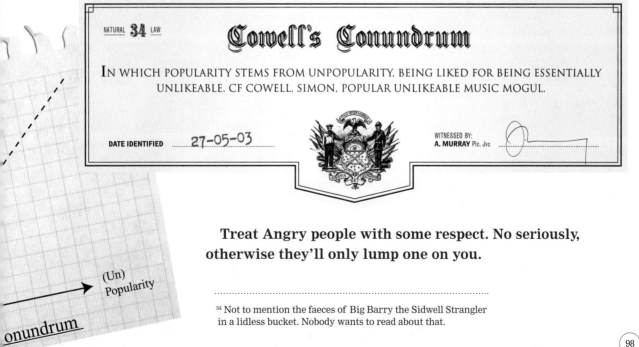

NATURAL **34** LAW

Cowell's Conundrum

In which popularity stems from unpopularity, being liked for being essentially unlikeable. CF Cowell, Simon, popular unlikeable music mogul.

DATE IDENTIFIED ......27-05-03......

WITNESSED BY:
A. MURRAY Plc. Jvc

(Un) Popularity

onundrum

Treat Angry people with some respect. No seriously, otherwise they'll only lump one on you.

[54] Not to mention the faeces of Big Barry the Sidwell Strangler in a lidless bucket. Nobody wants to read about that.

NG
AD
RE

This seemed like such a good idea at the time,
BANG HEAD HERE, but thanks to the middle
of the bloody book it doesn't work, which is just
fuelling further anger... ARGHH. Happy Now?

6 Help Yourself to Crippling Debt

Right now as you read this book we are of course staring the financial abyss in the face[55]. And the big difference between this and every other news story is this one hasn't gone away, so it must be real and not some cooked-up scare-the-punters-to-get-the-punters-to-watch-the-news piece of news.

It affects you and me, the man on the street, the woman in the kitchen. But the big mystery with the Credit Crunch is no one understands it, least of all the banks. In this country alone £200 billion has vanished. Gone. Disappeared. Evaporated. Almost as if it was never there. Almost as if your crummy house you were relying on selling at ludicrous mark up wasn't worth it after all[56].

Where could £200 billion go (apart from into comedy genius Ricky Gervais's bank account)? And let's face it banks have one job, to look after your money. That's all they have to do – put the money in the safe, shut the door, sit a bloke with a dog down next to the door on a metal chair. Their running costs are what? Sandwiches and dog food. They didn't spend £200 billion on sandwiches and dog food now did they? (Unless "Sir" Fred Goodwin is planning to spend his retirement walking the dog and picnicking). No, they spunked it, basically. In Iceland. Like a tramp scrounging for stale frozen food. Which is a bleak thought.

So the banks are running round like headless chickens, though headless chickens must at least know they have no head, and went to

MP'S EXPENSES

LOSE MONEY

GOVERN

MORE BANKS

HEALTH & SAFETY

OUR

---

[55] And I have to say that makes me appreciate you buying it even more. I have to say that.
[56] Although it is all the banks' fault, obviously, some of this happened because of the breakdown of traditional capitalism, i.e. people started trusting estate agents and believing what they said. Predict that, Karl Marx!

the government for help. Just the way we're not allowed to: if I borrow too much and blow it out of my arse spectacularly on a horse (Pub Fire # 3) the government say tough shit pal, too bad, dole queue, now! (though due to Pub Fire # 2 and my continued non-existence I can't sign on). But the banks are different, because if the government doesn't help we're told the whole thing will all go horribly wrong, even though they've only gone to the government because it's all gone horribly wrong.

So Gordon Brown gets out a chequebook and writes the banks a cheque for £200 billion pounds (about five World War Twos worth). But before we discuss whether he's done the right thing or not let's just consider something. Who's money is it the banks have lost? Is it their money? No, of course not, it's **OUR** money. They're meant to look after **OUR** money. **OUR** money. **OURS**. As in not theirs. As in no one else's. Least of all theirs. So, let's scroll back to Gordon Brown and his chequebook. Because it's not his chequebook, is it? Not really. It's **OURS**. The cheque of £200 billion is £200 billion of **OUR** money. Is it his money? No. it's **OURS**. **OUR** money. So he's replacing **OUR** money that the banks lost with **OUR** money. But he hasn't got £200 billion of **OUR** money, has he, because he's spent it on health and safety and the 2012 Olympics. So what he's done is he's borrowed £200 billion from another bank, which is of course **OUR** money. So he's borrowing **OUR** money to replace **OUR** money to replace **OUR** money. And then to pay off the loan he's got to raise taxes, and whose money is the tax? It's **OUR** money. So he's taking **OUR** money to replace **OUR** money to replace **OUR** money to replace **OUR** money. And this whole time him and his pals are claiming expenses and whose money is that? **OUR** money. So it's **OUR** money, **OUR** money, **OUR** money, **OUR** money, **OUR** money. Wankers.

Now, if I can figure out that this doesn't add up, and I am but a humble publican, then how can those in charge of the monies not spot it? Is it because bottom line, no one – not even the blokes who are lining their pockets with **OUR** money – knows what they're doing? That would seem to be the only logical explanation.

BANKS

OLYMPICS

N T

RAISE
TAXES

MONEY

But fortunately for you, I do know what I'm doing, and trust me, if there's absolutely no other way out, if you have exhausted absolutely every other option, as a matter of absolutely the last resort, you could always do what I do and burn down the pub and claim the insurance. Four times I've done it now, and it's like being born again, I'm telling you.

6.1 Help Yourself to Deal with Debt

It's a scam, obviously. It's a con, it's a hustle, like that thing about hustlers on the telly (I forget the name of it) only without The Man From UNCLE[57] getting involved. Needless to say, like all good cons it requires planning, creativity, strategy, keeping yer marff shut, nerve and an accelerant that doesn't smell. ("That stuff you squirt on barbecues? Yes, I do use it to clean the carpet, Mr Sun Alliance..." – practise saying that).

Now this isn't absolutely foolproof. The third time I burned my pub down I realised after the dust, soot and ash had settled that I was still seventy G in the bloody hole, so had to burn down a friend's place as well and split the winnings (he asked for what we call a "non fatal" – he didn't want to fake his death on account of actually loving his wife – yeah, I know!). The thing to watch out for is the tipping point, the point where you realise that your pub is worth more to you as a smouldering ruin than it is as a going concern. Then it just might be time for another little deep fat fryer mishap.

[57] Napoleon Solo, which is surely French for having a *Think*. Perhaps with a brandy on the go.

Pubsure

FORM 568ML

~~E ONLY~~

	SECTION A. ACCOUNT INFORMATION		

1. SEX
Landlord [X]   Landlady [ ]   No thanks, I'm British [ ]

2. NAME
ALAN MURRAY

3. ADDRESS
20 RUGBY STREET

4. POSTCODE
WC1N 3QZ

5. CITY
LONDON

6. TELEPHONE
0207 061 378

7. EMAIL (ONLY REQUIRED IF YOU OWN A PONCY WINE BAR)

9. NAME OF PUB
KING GEORGE ~~IV & V~~ VI

10. TYPE OF PUB
English Pub [X]   Gastro Pub [ ]   Wine Bar [ ]

11. FOOD SERVED
Scratchings [X]   Nuts [X]   Gourmet [ ]

12. DATE OF CLAIM
23 11 2009

13. SIGNATURE

SECTION B. REASON FOR CLAIM

1. TYPE OF INCIDENT
Flood [ ]   Fire [X]   Burgurlary [ ]   Vandalism [ ]   Other [ ]

2. CAUSE OF INCIDENT
Nature [ ]   Criminal [ ]   Accidental [ ]   Electrical [X]

3. PLEASE ELABORATE

Must have been something electrical, maybe a fault with one of the 15 new plasma screens I just hand installed.

4. EMERGENCY SERVICES
Police [X]   Fire [X]   Ambulance [ ]

5. WAS THERE CASH AT THE PROPERTY?
Yes [X]   No [ ]

6. HOW MUCH? (PLEASE PROVIDE EVIDENCE OF CHARRED COINAGE)
£35,000

7. PRICELESS OIL PAINTINGS AT THE PROPERTY?
Yes [X]   No [ ]

8. PLEASE DETAIL

Horseracing in Longchamps, Degas
(on loan from Boston Museum of Fine Art)
Le déjeuner sur l'herbe, Manet
(on loan from Musée d'Orsay Paris)

DO NOT WRITE BELOW THIS LINE

Pubsure

OFFICIAL USE ONLY

SECTION B. CONTINUED

9. PLEASE LIST ANY OTHER PRICELESS POSSESSIONS DESTROYED

20 dvd players

15 giant plasma screen

Ceramic Flanimals Collection in
    original packaging

Stradivarius Violin

Collection of Rolex Watches

Classic Cars stored in underground parking:

1961 Ferrari 250 GT,

1964 Ferrari 250 LM

SECTION C. LIFE INSURANCE CLAIM

THIS SECTION ONLY NEEDS TO BE COMPLETE IF THE POLICY HOLDER HAS DIED

1. OTHER INSURED'S NAME	2. OTHER INSURED'S DATE OF BIRTH
Most people just call me Al	20 / 05 / 1976

3. CAUSE OF DEATH

Nature ☐   Electrical ☒   Accidental ☐   Criminal ☐

4. PLEASE ELABORATE

It was closing time and I heard a loud bang in the cellars. I went to check, and the rest as they say, is history.

5. WITNESSES

Steve (the one with the funny toenail)

Steve (Steve's best mate)

Alan (Nothing to do with Steve)

7. NEXT OF KIN / BENEFICIARY

MR ANDREW MURRAY
(identical twin brother)

Al's Insurance Tips

3 When claiming the money for rebuilding the pub, remember that your old pub, the one that: "Just went up in flames, Officer", contained lots and lots of unbelievably expensive gear. Just to bump the figures up a bit.

4 If you are faking your own death to make a fresh start, remember to change your life insurance policy so that you can claim it yourself under an alias after your fake death. Do not leave it in your ex-wife's name so she can use the unexpected windfall to buy a wine bar in France and ensure that you don't see your son for the next eight years (and counting), for example.

5 Bear in mind that after your fresh start it will be virtually impossible to apply for a passport and indulge in foreign travel.

DO NOT WRITE BELOW THIS LINE

6.2 Help Yourself to Deal with Debt #2
Invent Your Own Flanimals

Now, if one day you find yourself really in the hole – maybe you had a punt on the stock market, impressed by Howard off of the Halifax ads, and invested all your money in the bloody Halifax just before they wiped billions off the value of the bloody thing, or maybe you put it all on Henman to win Wimbledon 'cos some bloke told you it was "definitely his year", not realising that he meant it was definitely his year to retire from the sport altogether, I don't know. We all have our sob stories, I'm sure. But if you find yourself up to your neck in debt, and you can't face burning the pub down so soon after the last one, and anyway the loss adjuster's been in a couple of times recently and you think he might be staking you out, well, there is another way.

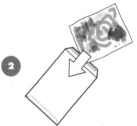

Now, this is pretty much foolproof, and all you really need is a rainy afternoon when there's nothing on the telly. The idea, basically, is this. You know those books Ricky Gervais has done, about some creatures he's made up called *Flanimals*? Just do that. He's a genius. We are lucky to live in such times.

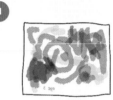

Bear in mind first off that you can't call your thing *Flanimals*, it's already called that. There are many other possibilities, though. How about *Badimals*? Or *Sadimals*? Or *Fleatures*, yeah, that one's good. The other one you can't have, by the way, is *Flonsters*, 'cos that's what my one's called.

Anyway, dead simple, get your mate's kid to draw up some stupid looking potato-faced blobs, give the buggers daft names, then toss off a couple of lines about how one lives in a tree and one lives in a pond

How to make a million

blah blah, whatever, don't worry about that. Then, stick Ricky Gervais's name on it, send it to ITV, and (and this is the important part) make sure you put *your address* on the envelope for them to send the cheques to. Then ITV, they'll take care of animating it, don't worry, although that part may take several years. Meanwhile you hire a tame nerd to set up a website where you can flog off hand-crafted miniature ceramic models for £27.99 apiece, also made by mate's kids: students will lap this stuff up regardless. Repeat once a year every year in time for Christmas[58,] and maybe you'll never have to set fire to your pub again.

---

[58] Now all you've got to do is sit back and count it as it comes pouring in, or roll around in it shouting "mine all mine!", or bag it up and hide it under the bed, convert it into bullion and put it in safe deposit box, pay someone to write good reviews for the dust cover of *Flonsters In Space 3*, or take it to the Isle of Man in a suitcase in an attempt to get the money overseas, hide it in the oven, hide it in the freezer, bury it at the bottom of the garden in an old ammunition case, keep it at the top of a bookshelf in a shoe box humorously labelled "tax documents", have a suit made of fifty pound notes, wipe your arse with fivers, cover a woman with gold just to see what happens, tell yourself that this is what Spike Milligan would be doing if he were still alive and yes it is a shame he didn't make the kind of money I am, put a real hotel on Mayfair, buy a hospital a kidney machine they can't afford to run, convert it into dollars and back into pounds again, use it to lure Carol Vorderman into getting into debt herself, give some to Richard Branson just to see what he does with it (he'll invest it in Virgin), use it to make friends with David Bowie, insure yourself for a cool billion then fake your own death and collect whole new pile of cash under assumed identity, buy Queen, go on about how you haven't sold out and Flonsters was what it was all leading up to all along (yet despite not having sold out somehow you have a giant house in central London), piss it away slowly over a really long period of time taking holidays in luxurious places in between pissing it away at home, buy one huge uncut diamond and sit next to it laughing in an otherwise empty mansion, use it to destroy the credibility of the Euro. I don't know it's up to you, the thing is you'll have plenty of time to think of what to do with the money seeing as getting it required so little thought and effort.

Case History #3

Name	Fran & Barry's boys
Age	13, 11 & 7
Sex	Male

Subject: My three nephews. I say nephews, actually they're my uncle Barrie's daughter Fran's boys, and Barrie isn't really my uncle any more than I am theirs, but they needed a strong male role model when their Dad decided to start a new life in Rhyl as a really desperately plain woman, and, well, yours truly stepped up to the oche. I mean, Rhyl, I ask you...

Description: Small & weird looking.

Problem: The impetuousness and impatience of youth. They know what they want to do with their lives, you see. They want to be publicans, just like their uncle-who's-not-really-their-uncle. It's beautiful, in many ways, it's enough to bring a tear to my eye, and a Union Jack hanky from my pocket to dab it away with. Trouble is they just can't wait. They know, you see, that I was a publican at thirteen[59], so why should they bother with sums, and reading, and writing, when all they want to be dealing with is crisps, nuts and scratchings. Anyway, last Christmas they built a one eighth-scale pub entirely out of Lego, and the really annoying thing was it had a carvery and everything, with a sneezeguard made from clear bricks. My real pub hasn't even got a carvery. That's the dream. These boys are living the dream, only they're living it in Lego form. I need to get them back to school, you get me? Although God knows my heart isn't in it. I myself graduated from the University of Life[60] and it didn't do me any harm. The point is, though, that their Mum, Uncle Barrie's daughter, is going to kill me if they don't knock it off soon. So I tell them, "Don't wish your lives away, boys. Your time will come. These happy innocent sunlit years are for conkers and chopper bikes, spacehoppers and shoplifting[61]. The time to serve will be here soon enough." But the oldest one just looks at me and says: "We want to be just like you, Uncle Guv, just like you." Then the other two join in. "Just like you, just like you..." It's like sodding Village of the Damned in there some nights, I'm telling you.

Solution: I don't know what the hell to do with the poor little sods. They're clearly not all there.

Prescription: They have a dream. You can't blame them, really, can you?

[59] See MY MISERABLE LIFE by Al Murray the Pub Landlord.
[60] Also Landlord Academy. I have a diploma.
[61] Please shoplift responsibly, kids.

Signed

MUGGINS

∼ WILLIAM ARTHUR WARD ∼

"A pinch of praise is worth a pound of scorn.
A dash of encouragement is more helpful than a dipper
of pessimism. A cup of kindness is better than a
cupboard of criticism."

Right, where do I start with this nonsensical waste of English language?
What is this mate? A recipe[62]? And what's a dipper? A chicken dipper,
do you mean? A chicken dipper of pessimism? You can tell he's American
by the fact he's measuring stuff in cups and cupboards, the fool. What's
wrong with pints and half pints, and quarter pints? The worst part is not
the fact that this bloke sounds uncannily like somewhere I stayed
overnight after I'd had a Hoover attachment removed (long story), it's
that he actually did this for a living. If someone said: "Go and see Bill
with that problem you're having with your missus, he's full of loads of
good advice", and I did, and he said this to me, the only measurement
he'd be left with was a fistful of rage.

[62]See COOK YOURSELF BRITISH, by Al Murray the Pub Landlord.

Where Darwin Went Wrong

You know the naturalist[63] Charles Darwin right? The chap who looks a bit like Uncle Albert from *Only Fools and Horses*[64] going to a fancy dress party as a poorly-judged comedy Rabbi? Yeah, that's right, him. Well, in his day, he (that's Darwin, not Uncle Albert) had some

Fig 1. Darwin, what a funny old man

very revolutionary ideas about how we got here and what's what etc. He reckoned we evolved from apes and through a thing called Natural Selection came to be the sophisticated beasts we are today[65].

At the time this caused a load of hoo-hah with the Church, because he basically blew thousands of years of religious bla-bla out of the water with some utterly plausible explanations of things. The problem with the Church is that they don't like utterly plausible explanations of things. In fact the more ludicrous and inexplicable the explanation

[63] Just because he liked to go to them nudist beaches he never got taken as seriously as he should have.
[64] There wasn't a lot to laugh at back in the late eighties/early nineties, and this was one of them.
[65] Some of us, anyway.

the better it is for them: people coming back from the dead, someone parting an entire ocean, someone having the ability to turn water into wine and yet not opening a wine bar, and forty days and nights of solid rain in the Middle East, to name but a few of their faves.

The Church has since apologised to Darwin some one-hundred and fifty years later, but to be honest it's a bit late lads, you've already knocked his theoretical pint over without buying him another one. What good is a theoretical pint to a dead man? Actually what's the use in a theoretical pint? Almost as pointless as the virtual pub we had on the show last year. Timewasters. <u>You can't download scratchings, and until you can I'm not interested.</u>

Charles Darwin's big idea was called Evolution, of course. It depends on a process he described as the Survival of the Fittest, whereby the Fittest would be the ones who ensured that their extremely fit DNA[66] was passed on to future generations, whilst the feebler and stupider specimens of a species would not succeed in doing this to such a great extent, thus gradually weeding themselves out.

Fig 2. There is but a dream

Charles lived in the nineteenth century, before the invention of the housing estate, which was to knock his precious theory into a cocked hat. Nowadays your average housing estate inhabitant has maybe nine children by ten different fathers (there's always one she's not a hundred per cent sure about), and what's more she has begun this process at the age of about sixteen.

....

[66] Invented years after Darwin croaked by a double act called Watson and Crick, who were big for a while before Morecambe and Wise came along. When they showed their new invention to all the other scientists for the first time they stood on either side of it and pulled the black silk cloth off the top, both going "Da-naaah!", which is how it got its name. True story.

This means she's
more than likely
a grandmother by about thirty
three or thirty four, and a great-grandmother by
fifty. As a result the DNA (and of course the DSS) has been spread
across four generations inside half a century, to a pool of maybe
eighty individuals, all of whom are hell bent on carrying on the
same process as hard and as fast as possible. After all, they'll
all want council flats too, especially with the housing market the
way it is now, it's only Common Sense.

And what have the Fittest been up to all this time, eh? Well,
Angelina Jolie has done her best, but she's been adopting too,
which is all well and good but, for the purposes of this argument,
is merely spending precious nurturing on somebody else's DNA.
Madonna? Same thing. Halle Berry has had one kid. Myleene's had
one. Elizabeth Hurley? Hasn't had any at all yet.

If they're not careful the Fittest are going to find themselves
outnumbered in short order, and they're going to find that
evolution has gone into reverse, which means that in a generation
or two we can expect to start seeing Morlocks about the place. I'm
not altogether sure that hasn't already started happening...

Now then, if we have really been adapting for the last billion,
squillion years, that means we are still changing, right?
This is the bit I'm worried about.

Let's look at the demise of the
tail. We all used to have tails,
but as Darwin points out we
lost them due to the fact we no
longer had any use for them, on
account of not living in trees
any more. But who was the first

person to lose his tail? I can just picture the scene: Steve walks into the pub and all the lads say hello and offer him a pint etc. All's well until Geoff points out Steve has woken up without his tail. They all laugh and point at him with their fifteen fingers, and he's a total laughing stock and is subsequently thrown out of not only the pub, but the footy, darts and pool team. A tragic scenario. Doubly tragic when you imagine all the fit women who then wouldn't want to get off with him, preferring to breed with the blokes who still had their tails like normal people. Not Geoff, obviously, because of the foot odour thing, but generally speaking.

Anyway, what concerns me is not just that I seem to have inadvertently disproved Evolution, but also this talk of <u>things falling off as a result of non-use.</u> You know what I'm getting at. It's been a year, that's what I'm saying. A year-long drought, with no end in sight. I know that Darwin was talking about extremely long timescales and everything, but a year seems like a bloody eternity right now. Now, maybe it is the future of mankind to evolve into a completely cockless state. Maybe it is. I just don't want to be the first, that's my point. Also, how will this new breed of cockless men manage to pass on their DNA to the Fittest? Haven't thought of that one, have you Darwin, you time waster?

Fig 4: Murray's Theory of Evolution: it's not pretty.

Here come the...

Fl0nsters!

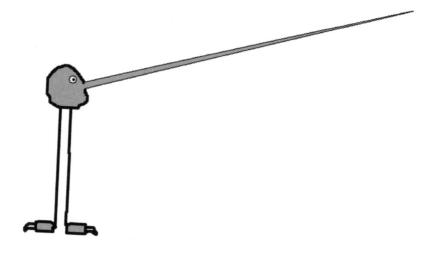

The Frumptious Poklespike
The deadly enemy of the one that looks like a big eye.

7 Help Yourself to Success

I'm not one of these so-called lifestyle gurus who makes extravagant claims that they can change your life and make you Successful. All I'm saying is if you follow my advice, this Help Yourself[67] Guide to Success that I've put together will definitely Help You to Help Yourself[68] be Successful. Definitely. So read on.

7.1 Success is a State Of Mind

"Nothing succeeds like Success", the saying goes. You'd hope so, wouldn't you, because if Success itself is failing then what chance have the rest of us got, eh? Who comes up with these sayings? They need to start thinking them through.

The trouble with Success is that it's a bit like the very first time someone ironed a shirt – suddenly all the other shirts looked messy and like they needed ironing. In the same way once someone was Successful, it made everybody else look like a complete loser. Up till that point there was no such thing as a loser, but nowadays nobody wants to be one. Now everybody feels like they needs some Success.

But what *is* Success? Everyone has their own Success barometer, don't they? Mine usually points at "Stormy", however hard I tap it. I wonder what the Success barometer of the bloke who invented the barometer looked like. In many ways, that bloke who invented the barometer's Success barometer was probably the second

[67] £1,471 Garden Costs, **James Arbuthnot MP (Cons)**
[68] £2,000 to replace a leaking pipe under his tennis court, **Oliver Letwin MP (Cons)**

successfully working barometer, after the first actual barometer, which he himself had successfully invented.

For me, Success is getting through a busy Friday night unscathed. Actually, lately Success for me is an even vaguely busy Friday night full stop. It's all I can do not to dip into the carvery fund to buy myself a kebab. What I'm trying to say is Success is relative. In my case that relative is my brother, who broke my family's heart and opened up a wine bar. I don't know if it's a Success or not, but since he's been shunned he's got out of sending Christmas and birthday cards, so there's a modicum of Success there if you want to look at it that way.

We live in a World where even the government seems to be worried about whether we're happy or not – which is odd seeing as their entire job is to piss us all off, surely – and the entire world is utterly hung up on whether it is a Success or not.

7.2 *Showing Off*

Let's start by trying to agree on what Success is. How do you spot Success? What makes you point at one bloke and say: "He's a Success!", while you will look at the next bloke and make an "L" on your forehead with your fingers, and jut out your bottom lip at him, going: "Du-u-u-u-uh! Lo-o-o-oser!"

Fig. 1. I always wondered what this meant

For some people – well, for most people, probably – Success is first and foremost all about Money. Not just having Money, either, but flashing it about where everyone else can see it and feel jealous of you. This is what is called Conspicuous Consumption. This just shows you how times have changed – a hundred years ago conspicuous consumption would be someone who'd really very obviously got Tuberculosis, hacking cough, pale face, weeping eyes, bloodied handkerchief, general borrowed-time look.

Now that we live in a consumer society and this once great nation relies on shopping[69] to feel better about itself rather than heroic rearguard actions by men in red coats against giant swarming hordes of people who we haven't sold rifles to yet, everyone Consumes Conspicuously. This is why you now see an endless parade of herberts dressed in clothes with the labels on, so we can all see exactly how much they spent and on what, and the manufacturers get to use them as an advertising hoarding in return. The next step, in Broken Credit Crunch Britain, will be designer tops where the price is actually part of the design. "This sweatshirt cost £44.99", kind of style, the fashion equivalent of waving your wad at the world.

NATURAL **64** LAW

Norton's Law

GUIDE TO UNDERSTANDING THE WORLD

$E = C$, WITH E BEING ENTENDRE, AND C REPRESENTING COMEDY. NORTON'S LAW EMPLOYS NORTONIAN PHYSICS, AND IS A MODERN REDUCTION OF HOWERD'S WAY, ($2E=C$) WHICH STATES THAT IN ORDER TO PROVIDE COMEDY EACH ENTENDRE MUST BE DOUBLED.

DATE IDENTIFIED   30-11-03

WITNESSED BY:
A. MURRAY Plc. Jvc

Rich people splash out on great big boats, allowing them to be seasick under penthouse conditions, but the point is the big shiny yacht tells you the bloke on board is successful at what he does, whether it's arms dealing, playing poker, making movies, selling grommets or supplying Woolies with those fried egg sweets (someone cornered that market, and whoever he was he's rolling in it; Pick'n'Mix, it was a licence to print money[70]), and if the yacht's parked up in Monaco for the Grand Prix then you can be sure he's shifted loads of those fried eggs.

You could even say plastic surgery – and we all know how expensive that is[71] – is a form of Conspicuous Consumption. The more ironed the

---

[69] This has led to the absurd spectacle of shops being open at four in the morning, because they say there's demand from people who want to buy cornflakes at four in the morning. Though really, are those the sort of people whose demands we should be giving in to in Great Britain today?
[70] Shafted now, though, aren't you mate? Eh?
[71] How long before some rich woman gets the idea of having the price of her plastic surgery stamped on her head for all to see? It's coming…

fifty-something woman's face looks the more money she must have spent or had spent on her. We were given eyebrows for a reason[72], and they're where they are because that's where they're supposed to be[73]. They don't belong in a surgeon's incinerator bin along with the bits of your nose you don't like and that bit of tummy you thought you'd have tucked. Besides, when you die, will you be reunited with these lopped off parts when you get to Heaven? No of course not, because you're going to Hell. Tamper with God's Creation at your peril, vain women.

Fig. 2. Sue the surgeon!

Where was I? Oh yeah. So what do we reckon? Having lots of dough to splash about on stuff – is that Success?

7.3 Saturday Night Success

We live in a society nowadays where every Saturday night we see a seemingly interminable parade of no-marks and chancers apparently having Success beyond their wildest dreams.

That's before we even get to *The Lottery*. Christ, every week some bloody unemployable chump suddenly finds himself with a giant cheque for 14 million quid in his hands, and before you know it he's got a pool, and a roller, and a yacht, and he looks for all the world like a Success, but all he's actually done with his life is mooched a quid off of the woman who he's since abandoned and who is now suing him for half, and he's managed to shuffle down to the petrol station in his slippers to buy a piece of paper which he hopes against hope will lift him out of the noxious pit of despair in which he's been wallowing.

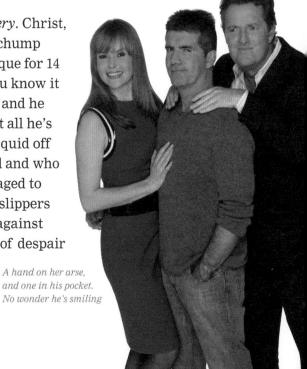

A hand on her arse, and one in his pocket. No wonder he's smiling

[72] Though God alone knows what it might be.
[73] Nope, still no idea. If anyone says they know they're probably guessing, or at best making it up.

Fig. 3. Coming soon?

I have only ever had a winning ticket once. I think it was a winning ticket, anyway. Unfortunately between my buying it and the numbers actually being announced it went up in flames during a pub conflagration for insurance purposes, which ironically would have been rendered completely unnecessary by the winnings. And I could have had a carvery, probably. Fate is a fickle mistress, that's for sure. With a wide variety of virulent sexually transmitted diseases.

The point is this: one of the key ways in which we measure Success in this celebrity-powered age is Fame. The thing is, nowadays you don't actually have to do much to get Fame. Look at Saturday nights, that's all you've got to do. If it isn't the *X Factor* it's *I'd Do Anything*, if it's not *Britain's Got Talent* it's *Any Dream Will Do* or that Eurovision thing. All you have to do is pitch up and be not quite as good at singing as the people who are already doing it professionally, and suddenly the world seems to be your oyster, and no one minds if you cry on telly until snot comes out of your nose.

To me, there is something not particularly British about all that. I look at it, and I think this is how Americans go on. It's no coincidence that Simon Cowell and Piers Morgan have been over there picking up tips on how to wind people up to a frenzy of Success neediness.

The message of these programmes seems to be that Anyone Can Do Anything. Anyone can be a Success, all they have to do is want it enough, and it will definitely definitely happen, and they can be elevated from the pit by the divine hand of Cowell (while his other hand is dipping into your back pocket and taking 75 per cent).

Actually, though, the real message of these shows is the opposite one. It is this: it is actually unreasonable to expect Success. Not everybody can be Successful. In fact hardly anybody can. And in order for you to be Successful, everybody else has to be a Loser. That's the Maths. Not everybody can be Nancy. Just the winner of that show, and possibly Graham Norton.

For every Success there must be a Loser. Think about that. It's charming, isn't it? This means that if you are striving hard to achieve your ambition, you are also deliberately trying to rub some other poor bugger's nose in it. How does that make you feel? Does it make you want to roar like a tiger? Or do you feel like a bit of a shit?

Fig. 4. Take your pick

With my Help Yourself[74] Guide to Success I will show you how everyone can be a Success. That's right, you heard me. Everyone can be a Success. It's not between you and the next bloke. He can be a Success too. You don't have to grind his face into the gravel[75].

So let's get on with it.

....

[74] Pints of milk, fluffy dusters and chocolate biscuits, **Chris Huhne MP (Lib Dem)**
[75] Unless he's looked at your pint.

First a bit of a quiz, and I want you to think about this carefully.

Which of these things would you regard as a Success? You can put ticks or crosses alongside them if you want, but you should be aware that this will affect the resale value of the book. In fact, it occurs to me that I don't want you reselling it, do I, I want you having to buy another one, so tick-and cross away. Be my guest.

7.4 Success Quiz

How do you measure Success? Are these things Success? What do you reckon?

☺ ☺ ☹ Getting Gold at the 2012 Olympics (why did we take that on, it's only going to end in tears)?

☺ ☺ ☹ Winning the F1?

☺ ☺ ☹ Winning the Grand National?

☺ ☺ ☹ Winning the *X Factor* (ask Steve Brookstein that one)?

☺ ☺ ☹ Making a million before you're 21?

☺ ☺ ☹ Making a million before you're 30?

☺ ☺ ☹ Making a million before you're 40?

☺ ☺ ☹ Making a million before you're 50?

☺ ☺ ☹ Making a million before you're 60? (not so impressive that one)

☺ ☺ ☹ Making a million before you're 70? (leaving it a little in the day aren't you?)

☺ ☺ ☹ Making a million before you're 80? (you're wasting everyone's time with that one pal, knock it off)

☺ ☺ ☹ Playing for your country at international level – not that the blokes who do these days seem to give a toss about that anyway?

☺ ☺ ☹ Getting a high-score on Final Carnage 6? (grow up)[76]

[76] The computer was originally invented to defeat the Germans in World War II, which is why the only games it's alright for you to play on it are World War II games in which you defeat the Germans.

123

☺ ☺ ☹ Having your letter to the local paper complaining about the new noise restrictions in the street which means the punters who used to take it outside to fight now have to fight inside the pub and it's resulted in three copper-topped tables with the hammered effect being broken, and I've had to cannibalise them to make one that doesn't wobble, published?

Go on, eat it!

Aim , fire

☺ ☺ ☹ Stuffing 42 grapes into your gob?

☺ ☺ ☹ Stuffing 43 grapes into your gob?
(Ha! Suffer, Mr 42-grape ambition guy!)

☺ ☺ ☹ Stuffing 44 grapes into your … forget it.

☺ ☺ ☹ Flipping a pancake successfully?

☺ ☺ ☹ Getting to watch what you want this evening,
not *Britain's Next Top Model*?

☺ ☺ ☹ Holding your breath for a minute and a half?

☺ ☺ ☹ Downing a pint in one?

☺ ☺ ☹ Flicking the bogey into the bin?

☺ ☺ ☹ Getting all the chocolate off the Malteser before eating the middle?

☺ ☺ ☹ Finishing that book this year?

☺ ☺ ☹ Getting half an hour's clear time to sit on the bog and read *AutoTrader*?

It's not going to happen

She's not listening

☺ ☺ ☹ Cracking a lazy tired easy worn-out unimaginative joke about ginger people?

☺ ☺ ☹ Getting your tax return in on time though now you have to do the paperwork for them the lazy bastards, for some reason they fine you if it's late, when in fact they should pay you if it's on time?

☺ ☺ ☹ Thinking up five more Flanimals and then going for lunch?

☺ ☺ ☹ Stopping at four Flanimals because what's the point they'll sell anyway?

☺ ☺ ☹ Getting that promotion?

☺ ☺ ☹ Snogging the girl from accounts on the photocopier at the office Christmas party?[77]

☺ ☺ ☹ Going for a dump and the water not splashing your bum? (I think this is probably the first time this thorny topic has ever cropped up in a **Help Yourself** [78] book as a measure of success, but if you're in a rocky place or feeling down it can completely ruin your morning, and no matter what the rational half/third/quarter/eighth/sixteenth of your brain might tell you, that water isn't clean, even if it was before the turd splashed into it; the moment it did the water became dirty so there.)

And put your pencils down. Don't panic, there are no wrong answers apart from the wrong answers. We'll be checking back to your answers on this page in a bit.

---

[77] Aim higher, please.

[78] £40 – summons for the non-payment of council tax on a flat, **Lembit Opik MP (Lib Dem)**

7.5 Goals Goals Goals[79]

Hold pen 20cm above page and fire

Attempt 1   Attempt 2   Attempt 3

I've checked around the other Help Yourself gurus – not that I'm a guru, although I'm looking into it, I like the sound of tithing – and they all seem pretty much in agreement. The way to Success is to set your sights firmly on your Goals. Focus on your Goals, and Work Hard to reach them. And if you set yourself ambitious Goals, and strive to reach them 24/7, as these fellows seem keen on saying, then you are bound to be a Success, because even if you miss your Goal, you have still achieved something pretty great.

Now I haven't got fancy diplomas all over my wall from the University of Help Yourself,[80] but even I know a bit more about Goals than that. If you aim for a Goal and miss, then that's a Goal Kick, which is not great. Unless the keeper's got a touch, and then it's a corner, which is OK, but

Fig. 5. Congratulations, you're a loser (again)

[79] Not to be confused with the footy clips video GOALS GOALS GOALS GOALS, presented by Nick Hancock.
[80] £6,577 – cleaning, **Gordon Brown MP (Lab)**

not great either, especially if the oppo have a big brute of a centre half who wins everything in the air. Then suppose he nods it out of the box to their nippy little midfielder, who makes a mug of your last man, chips your keeper, and suddenly you're a Goal down. Then the final whistle goes before you can even kick off again and that's that. In short, you've aimed for your Goal, you've missed, and now you are a Loser.

We have now reached one of the key signposts on the Road to Success.

Goals are not the answer. Goals are the problem.

Remember that.

7.6   *Manage Your Expectations*

Fig. 6. Whatsherface

People today have unreasonable expectations of Success in my view. Ask most people in the street today what their ambition is and chances are they'll say: "I want to be a TV presenter". Admittedly, these are the sort of people who are prepared to answer personal questions about themselves on the television in the first place, so these are already bigheads and showoffs. And you might say it's not that difficult to be a television presenter, the bar is quite low. After all, you don't have to write anything, or invent anything, or create anything, you just have to stand in front of a camera and say whatever the concealed puppetmaster orders you to say. Easy. Even Vernon Kay can do it. Trouble is, though, becoming a television presenter is an unreasonable expectation for most people, because they have faces like smacked arses. And because there are far too many people who want the same thing and there isn't room for all of them. The telly isn't big enough to fit all their big heads on it.

BRAIN SPACE™ SAVER #4

Success tip:

High expectations and ambition take up valuable *BRAIN SPACE™*. Ditch these brain cluttering concepts and aim for the floor – you can't miss!

BRAIN SPACE™ saved: 78%

TOTAL BRAIN SPACE SAVED (%)

I am no champion athlete, I know that, I've come to terms with it. Therefore I know it's too much to ask of my body to get up and turn the television off. I would argue, though, that my use of the OFF button on the remote control counts as a resounding Success. The telly is off, and I haven't had to get up to do it. Result. So if you want to experience Success all you need to do is set clear and realisable goals that are within easy reach.

For instance, gentlemen, face it, you are never ever ever never ever ever never going to go to bed with Liz Hurley[81] so let it go (though the law of averages clearly states that you will at some time in your life, and sooner than you might think, be presented with the opportunity to turn down Jodie Marsh). This is only a realistic expectation if you're Hugh Grant, except he blew it big time, didn't he.

Fig. 7. Common visualising technique

....
[81] Not ever.

Mon	5	12	19	26
Tue	6	13	20	27
Wed	7	14	21	28
Thu	1	8	15	22	29
Fri	2	9	16	23	30
Sat	3	10	17	24	31
Sun	4	11	18	25	

Miss July

*Fig. 8. Here's a picture to help you with your
imaginings, though to be honest the internet's chockablock with them*

But if your goal is to *imagine* going to bed with Liz Hurley, well, what's stopping you from becoming a highly Successful imaginist? Only your own personal stamina and the risk of repetitive strain injury. It's that simple, set yourself a realistic goal and you can achieve Success.

Real Success comes from managing your expectations to a point where you can hardly fail. If you ticked the very last box on the Success Quiz a couple of pages back, then you are already well on the Road to Success. If you can get yourself to a state of mind where having a crap without the cold water splashing your backside counts as a Success then you will be a happy man, my friend.

To take another example from my own life: at the top of this section I seemingly set out to Help You to Help Yourselves to Success, but deep down I know that you lot aren't up to Helping Yourselves, so I simply managed my expectations and set myself the attainable goal of not really Helping You, and I'm pretty sure I have achieved it 100%.

To bring Success flooding into your daily life, try setting down some goals on a piece of paper. The key thing to remember is that the purpose of this is not to encourage yourself to achieve more, it is to set down things you're pretty sure are going to happen anyway, so that you can enjoy ticking them off later. Got it? Here is an example for you – you can even just copy it. How hard is that?

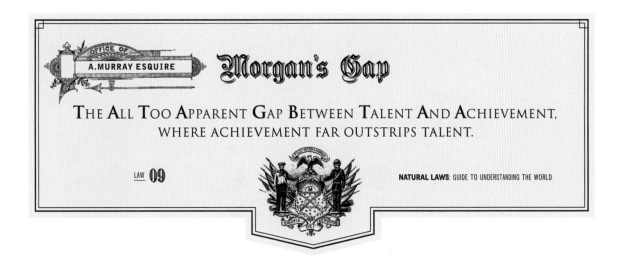

OFFICE OF

A. MURRAY ESQUIRE

Morgan's Gap

THE ALL TOO APPARENT GAP BETWEEN TALENT AND ACHIEVEMENT, WHERE ACHIEVEMENT FAR OUTSTRIPS TALENT.

LAW 09

NATURAL LAWS: GUIDE TO UNDERSTANDING THE WORLD

Easily attainable goals for your Steps To Success Programme:

✓ That third piece of unnecessary toast you shouldn't have – you can eat it! You're a Success!

✓ **That last dribble of whisky in the bottle – drink it! Win the battle with the bottle!**

✓ When you walk to the corner shop, whistle. Suddenly your life has a soundtrack. Nice one. That's Success.

✓ **Decide that today you are going to tell the boss to stick his bloody job up his fucking spotty arse but then realise that it might result in your being fired and you'll never get another job, not with your outdated qualifications, so decide against it and, lo, you have got through another week without being fired: you are a Success.**

✓ Buy some of those fried egg sweets from Woolies[82]: treat yourself, and you are contributing an important part of the bloke on his yacht in Monaco's Success – without you he would not Succeed, therefore you are the cause of his Success, therefore you yourself are Success (though it doesn't get you use of his yacht, admittedly[83]).

[82] Warning: you may have to look elsewhere on your gap-toothed High Street for a sweet fried egg outlet.
[83] He's probably selling it soon anyway.

It's that easy. Think up your own. Though what I'm not going to do is leave loads of pages blank like that chancer Gok Wan did in his last book for "*Notes*". Workshy, though you have to admire the footwork, don't you.

I have prepared a diagram (below) from my own copious life experience which I think demonstrates pretty conclusively that if you have Low Expectations you are more likely to be a Success than if you have High Expectations, and what's more that it's all going to end up the same anyway so it's not worth getting worked up about it.

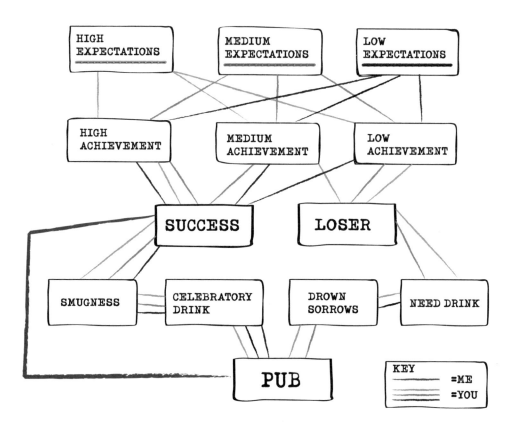

Case History #4

Name	Steve, Steve, Alan and Steve
Age	?,?,? and ?
Sex	Male

Subject: 1 loves Noel Edmons, 1 likes pigeons – need I say more

---

Description: Regular drinkers round my gaff. Assorted sizes, Steve's the funny one.

Problem: Well, they're at my pub all the time, and they can really stick it away, especially Steve. The problem is that their enthusiastic and voluminous drinking is restricting their personal development. I'm not saying they're not fully rounded individuals – that's definitely happening, don't worry about that – it's just that they could be doing so much more with their lives. Steve plays the trombone, for instance, and Steve breeds pigeons, while Steve has an uncanny sixth sense with the *Deal Or No Deal* bandit that must have an application in the job market somewhere. Alan, well, I reckon he just likes hanging round with Steve, while Steve and Steve just put up with him. Insofar as they work at all, it's in the "black economy" as it's called, by which I mean they sometimes put on fluorescent jackets then drive up to the roadworks on the motorway and nick tarmac.

Thing is, if they got proper jobs that would really eat into their drinking time. What if, God forbid, Steve got a job, and Steve's boss one night asked Steve to stay late, and by going home time Steve was just too knackered to come down the pub? No, no, it's far better that they come and let me cash their giros for them. After all, I'm pretty much banking on them to see me through this recession that everyone tells us is just around the corner.

Solution: If Steve, Steve, Alan and Steve cut back on their drinking time and channelled their energies into legitimate employment there's no doubt their prospects could improve dramatically, but from my point of view it ain't broke, so I'm not even going to try and fix it.

Prescription: **Signed**

Here come the...

Flonsters!

bits of beetroot

The Bootreet
Eats beetroot, which is how come it's purple.

1. THE SHRUG

You have a problem to deal with, something has taken a turn for the worse in your life, you're on a bit of a downer – well, so what? Shrug it off. Go on! Shrug! Worse things happen at sea! Lift your shoulders up an inch or two, and drop them back to their original starting position. Doesn't that feel better?

Fig. 1. What would I know?

Of course not. The Shrug belongs together with a range of other happy-clappy behaviours, most of which seem designed to make you appear like some kind of simpleton. Smile! Turn the other cheek! Use the phrase: "It's all part of life's rich tapestry!"

The problem I have with the Shrug is that it is a French invention, and what's more it is a key component of their language, largely replacing the need for them to come up with any new words since the Storming of the Bastille. We, the British, use the shrug to express, in effect, two sentiments only, these being "Oh well!" and "I don't know the answer to that." For a Frenchman the shrug can have any one or more of very nearly a thousand different meanings, many simultaneously. Here are a couple of whole conversations a Frenchman has shrugged at me:

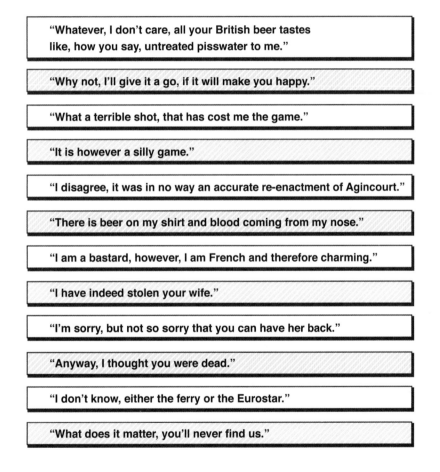

"Whatever, I don't care, all your British beer tastes like, how you say, untreated pisswater to me."

"Why not, I'll give it a go, if it will make you happy."

"What a terrible shot, that has cost me the game."

"It is however a silly game."

"I disagree, it was in no way an accurate re-enactment of Agincourt."

"There is beer on my shirt and blood coming from my nose."

"I am a bastard, however, I am French and therefore charming."

"I have indeed stolen your wife."

"I'm sorry, but not so sorry that you can have her back."

"Anyway, I thought you were dead."

"I don't know, either the ferry or the Eurostar."

"What does it matter, you'll never find us."

So whenever the subject of my ex-wife leaving me and running off with a Frenchman rears its ugly head, I find I am unable to Shrug it off. It reminds me of him. Thanks for bringing that up.

2. WORKING WITH YOUR HANDS

At times of great stress and mental turmoil it can be very therapeutic to work with your hands. In my trade, of course, working with my hands is very important. Pumping the pumps, lifting the kegs, and of course dispensing snacks. It's a very physical life, which is why I myself operate on such an even keel. All publicans do. And which is why, of course, I am able to point out, in a detached and disinterested yet caring way, areas in which you could improve your lives.

Fig. 2. I think I've finally go the hang of this.

You, on the other hand, probably work in an office somewhere, and there's someone who really gets your goat, or someone who never washes up the coffee cups, or someone who always pretends it wasn't them who jammed the photocopier and then tried to fix it with your brand new stapler. You probably have stress knots climbing up the back of your spine, and are ready to tear the head off the next person who says: "I'm going to need you to stay at least another hour – this photocopying really has to be done and stapled tonight", and piss down their neckholes directly into their lungs.

Well, one coping mechanism you might try is a little bit of Do It By Yourself, a little bit of a project you can do with your hands. A spice rack, perhaps, or a new shelf for knick-knacks[84]. You could even use a coping saw. And pretty soon the world will seem a better place. Or at worst ever so slightly tidier, with extra room in your cereals cupboard where the spices used to be. You'll have nicked your thumb doing that last bit, and the house will smell of sap, but you'll be coping, and that's what matters.

If you don't believe me, take a look at the Amish people. They've got so much to cope with, haven't they? Not allowed to shave, not allowed to watch the telly, only allowed to fornicate after marrying one of their own cousins, up at four for milking, not to mention those bloody silly hats. It's really not much of a life. But do they seem depressed, do they seem downhearted? No, they're too busy getting

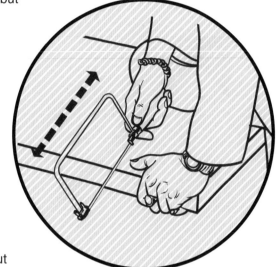

Fig. 3. Easy does it.

together for gigantic picnics, with heaving hampers and stuff, where they throw up a whole massive barn in a day, all pulling ropes together and hammering, some of them with their coping hammers, others sawing away with their coping saws. Inspiring stuff. Mental, but inspiring. Until the crooked cops turn up looking for the kid who knows too much, that is, and then Harrison Ford has to choke one of them in the grain silo and shoot the other one. Christ, think of the barns they must have had to build to cope with that little lot. It's not as if they even knew who Harrison Ford was, because they didn't have tellies, did they?

[84] See FLONSTERS! – THE MERCHANDISING CATALOGUE
or buy online at www.flonstermuchmoneysendnow.co.uk

3. THUMPING SOMEBODY

I'm not allowed to actually advocate this as a coping strategy for legal reasons, but we all know, don't we, that there are times when only thumping somebody will do. It doesn't necessarily have to be the bloke who's pissed you off, it could be some other poor git who's wandered into your orbit and put his coat on your chair while you were in the bog, or who's looked too longingly at your drink while he's trying to decide what to have, or maybe he's got a bit of a French name. Whatever the trigger is, you know that belting the living daylights out of him is the only thing that will make you feel better.

Fig. 4. Wear that, Frenchie!

But then there's the whole business of explaining yourself to the police, or to the wife, or to your mate who only brought the bloke into the pub in the first place "just to see if he'd like it". This is a whole other area of stuff you're going to have to cope with, and the thing is, I actually have a really good strategy for coping with this bit. I do! It's to start weeping and banging on and on about how you have unresolved issues, and how what you really need is therapy, and a shoulder to cry on. Try it – it's absolutely amazing what you can get away with. This country's fucked.

4. DRINKING

At the end of the day, though, whatever it is that's getting to you, nothing puts it right like the beautiful British pint. I would say that, though, wouldn't I, because that's what I'm selling[85]. Doesn't make it any less true, though, does it? So whatever it is that ails you, the ale will never fail you. Get yourself down to a beautiful British pub (preferably mine, the carvery fund's a bit low at the moment – it's a global trend, though, apparently) and get yourself sorted out. Until you can do that, here's a picture – that ought to hold you for the time being.

Fig. 5. Thank God you're still here. Don't ever leave me.

SO WHATEVER IT IS THAT AILS YOU, THE ALE WILL NEVER FAIL YOU

85 And FLONSTERS! – THE MERCHANDISING CATALOGUE
or buy online at www.flonstermuchmoneysendnow.co.uk

8 | Help Yourself to Food

(That heading is a bit confusing, isn't it? I mean, there isn't any food in this book for you to actually Help Yourself[86] to. I tried to get the publishers to lay that on but it was a logistical nightmare. The book would have had to have a sell-by date and be displayed in a refrigerated cabinet. More trouble than it's worth, basically, bloody Health and Safety. So, sorry about that. Anyway I just thought that when I eventually get myself a carvery – that's the dream – I could photocopy this page and make the heading into a laminated sign to go on the wall above the cutlery rack and the blister packs of ketchup. Save me a couple of bob, won't it...)

Now we come onto an area of life which we all experience, some more than others (you know who you are) and which I am in a position to help you to Help Yourself[87] to do better.

[86] £5,000 on furniture, avoided capital gains tax on £45,000, **Hazel Blears MP (Lab)**
[87] Thousands of pounds on renovating her second home in north London even though her main home is just 15 miles away, **Dawn Butler MP (Lab)**

Fig. 1. Oi! Just deliver the pizza!

I'm talking Food[88]

We all need it, grow it, dig it up, shop for it, order it over the phone and have it brought to us by a spotty kid on a moped, shoot it, harvest it, catch it in nets and hit it on the head with a club then rip its guts out with a small sharp knife, boil it in a bag, fry it, bake it, peel it, microwave it, broil it, slice it, dice it, sautée[89] it, slap it between two bits of sliced white and scoff it in front of the telly, and without it we'd be dead as the proverbial and reputedly very tasty dodo, but what do we really know about the stuff we're putting into our bodies?

8.1 You are what you eat

That's what they say, isn't it. "You are what you eat". It sounds obvious at first, but let's just think about that one for a moment. I mean, we are all of us a motley ragbag of bones, sinews, muscles, giblets, bile, blood, eyeballs, guts and brains, aren't we, and you wouldn't eat that if it was plonked down in front of you, would you? Not unless you were on holiday in Scotland and they told you it was haggis, and even then you probably wouldn't finish a whole one.

You are what you eat. If that was true, then I would look something like this...

---

[88] By which I mean I'm talking about food, not that I am a talking piece of food, except from the point of view of a loose tiger.
[89] French word.

Fried eggs.

Pork scratchings.
*Itchy skin & saltier
than excema*

Sausage.
*It's a Cumberland,
don't worry about that*

BEER

*I'd be made more or less entirely out of pork scratchings, and I know that isn't actually the
case because I haven't got a single hair on my body.*

Nutrition

Of all things to happen, a nutritionist came into my gaff the other week. It's not the start of a joke[90], it really happened. I took the opportunity to engage him in conversation, and, always eager to learn[91], I asked him what expert advice he might have for a man like me. He looked me up and down a bit, and then said:

"You sleep too much, you eat too much, you drink too much. You should get more exercise."

"Well," I said. "Exercise makes me tired. Exercise makes me hungry. Exercise makes me thirsty. If I get more exercise it will only make me sleep even more, eat even more, and drink even more. Some bloody expert you are."

I couldn't help noticing that despite subsisting almost entirely for the past four decades on snacks, bar food and beer, I am a picture of robust British healthiness, so I must be doing something right.

Fig. 2. A nutritionist at work.

This nutrition "expert", by contrast, spends his whole life weighing out bowls of pulses and taking mineral supplements, and he's the colour of six-day-old pants, with a hacking cough and a lingering aroma of the farmyard. So what does he know?

I offered him a complimentary peanut from the bowl on the bar, thought it might put a bit of colour in his cheeks, but he threw his hands up in horror.

---

[90] Such as: A nutritionist, a faith healer and a Scotsman came into my pub. I charged them four pounds seventy a pint. Makes me laugh, anyway...
[91] In order to pass off his knowledge as my own later.

Help Yourself...

"Don't you know that scientists have proved that each nut in that bowl will carry traces of twenty-eight different types of urine?"

"Well that's just nonsense," I said. "That bowl's only been out a fortnight, and we haven't had twenty-eight different people in here in that time."

Besides, how many different types of urine are there? Watery, very watery, dark but clear, dark but cloudy, steaming, blood-flecked, gushing, and smelling vaguely of toast. That's only eight. Scientists!

Food groups

Nutritionists – yes, it is a *job* now, apparently, I bet their fathers are proud of them – they like to divide foodstuffs up into groups, don't they? There's your carbohydrates, your proteins, your fibres, your vitamins, your minerals, your polyunsaturated fats, and your water (still, sparkling, tap), that sort of thing. Or else it's meats, grain, dairy, fruits, vegetables, nuts, pulses, seafood, other. They love it. They can make lists, and colour code them, and make charts showing how you're not getting enough of something or other (the nosey bastards) and that you need to eat loads more of the particular thing they happen to be able to sell you.

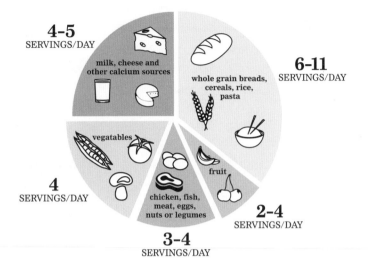

4-5
SERVINGS/DAY

milk, cheese and
other calcium sources

6-11
SERVINGS/DAY

whole grain breads,
cereals, rice,
pasta

vegatables

4
SERVINGS/DAY

chicken, fish,
meat, eggs,
nuts or legumes

fruit

2-4
SERVINGS/DAY

3-4
SERVINGS/DAY

All this seems to me to be complicating things unnecessarily.
Everyone knows there are only three sorts of foodstuffs, and
they are as follows:

STARTERS
MAINS
PUDDINGS

1 **THE STARTERS** group of foods can be broken into a few handy sub-groups, such as snacks, soups, sides, leftovers and special small portions of Mains available on request.

2 **MAINS** is the most substantial food group, and often the only one you need to make it through the day. Mains differs from the other major food groups in that it is the only one that can be served in a basket.

3 **PUDDINGS** as a group includes fruit (except melon, which is a Starter), Star Bars, ices and anything you find yourself thinking: "You know what? A bit of custard would go nicely with this..."

What's handy about this nutritional system is that it is remarkably flexible. Take, for example, a simple bowl of Coco Pops (grain, dairy). This can be a Starter – say for example at breakfast time while you're waiting for your full English to be ready. It can be a Pudding – obviously, with its sweet chocolatey goodness. And, at a pinch, it can be a Mains, for example when you've got absolutely nothing else in and the kebab shop is shut because kids put an old lady's motorised trike through the window trying to get at the cash out of the pinball machine. Kids!

Calories

You used to hear about calories all the time, didn't you? Women were especially agitated about them, for some reason, like they were the enemy. There would always be something called a "calorie-controlled diet", lurking in the background of the adverts somewhere, wouldn't there, as though the calories were telling the women what they could and couldn't eat, or bottles of pop with "less than one calorie per serving[92]". All calories are, though, are little holes in the enamel of your teeth, which... no, hang on a minute, Gary, that's cavities, I'm remembering the wrong advert... calories, right, yes, I've got it, they're energy, like the amount of fuel you put in a car to make it go. You've got to have calories, or else you'd grind to a halt. That's why it's ridiculous to have a calorie-controlled diet. You wouldn't put mileage-controlled petrol in your motor, would you? Of course you wouldn't, that would be madness.

Fill me up!

Helpful bacteria

You hear a lot of guff about how these little pots of yoghurt that women are told to eat when they feel bloated contain "helpful bacteria". What I want to know is just how helpful is it possible for bacteria to be? I mean, if a bacterium came to me wanting to help out in the pub, the first thing I'd have to say is: "How are you going to see over the bar, mate?" I suppose at a pinch he could give

---

[92] One serving = four swigs.

Helpful bacteria

a rowdy punter some sort of lurgy, but that would be bound to need an incubation period of some sort, by which time said rowdy punter would have tried his best, in more or less perfect health, to spread my nose across my face. So next time you hear someone banging on about "helpful bacteria", feel free to snort in a scathing fashion. Try to make sure snot doesn't come out of your nose and down your tie.

Cholesterol

Lots of the very best foods are packed with the life-giving goodness of cholesterol. Sausages, for instances, and fried eggs, and in fact most of the component parts of the All Day Breakfast. Cholesterol gets a bad press from the wafflers, who are trying to get it eliminated from daily life, much like smoking indoors. The word is made up of the *sterol* bit, which is a cross between **ster**oids and alco**hol** – food alcohol, what a bonus! – and the Greek word *chole*, which means bile. Which is why I myself look like a pissed-up angry weightlifter – my healthy cholesterol-packed diet.

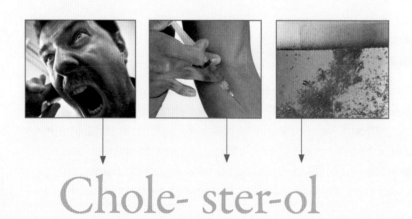

Chole- ster-ol

8.2 What you really need to know about food

The trouble with all that nutrition guff, the vitamins and the roughage, and the E numbers and the monosodium glutamate, is that it doesn't tell me what I really want to know. The things I really want to know about the stuff I'm bunging into my gob are as follows:

? *Will it send me to sleep?*

? *Will it make me fart?*

? *Will I be able to get it quickly?*

? *Will it make my breath smell?*

? *Will it help me soak up the booze?*

? *How will it affect the workings of my digestive system?*

To this end I have devised a system of ratings for each aspect of the world of foods. Let's take them one at a time.

This is a measurement to determine how tired a foodstuff will make you. To be honest, most reasonable-sized meals will give you winks, but some more than others. If your meal adds up to forty winks, then you will fall asleep. It's as simple as that. As an extreme example, a full Christmas turkey dinner with all the trimmings[93] is worth somewhere in the region of thirty-nine winks. You should just about be able to make it to the settee before *The Great Escape* starts, but if you then decide to indulge in an After Eight mint (one wink) you will then total forty winks and lapse into unconsciousness. Sushi on the other hand has a very low wink rating, as it is hard to nod off while perched precariously on a cold ceramic ring.

Certain things, not all of them food, can counteract the winks present in all foods. Coffee, for instance, provides negative winks, or anti-winks, as does an electric shock, treading on an upturned plug, or racking up a huge terrifying amount of debt without consolidating it into one single easy-to-manage loan.

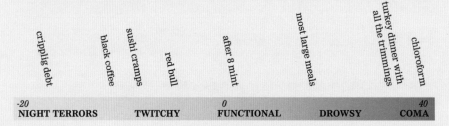

Fig 1. WINKS EXPLAINED

You can read as many books on food, nutrition and cookery as you like, but none of them will tell you the crucial information that could save you from a relationship-ending embarrassing social incident. No one minds when this happens in the privacy of your own home – just

---

[93] Always provide all the trimmings. No one ever asks for "some trimmings".

open a window or blame it on the dog. But what if you're meeting potential in-laws for the first time, you've gone round for a nice Sunday lunch, everything's going well, and then the winks start to kick in[94], and before you know it you're playing an arse trumpet involuntary on the old parpsichord.

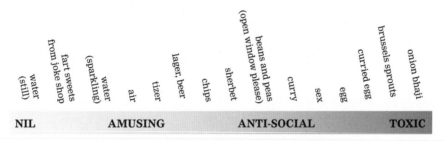

NIL   AMUSING   ANTI-SOCIAL   TOXIC

Fig 2. PARPSICORD EXPLAINED

Many vegetables have unusually high levels of parpicity, giving the lie to the old adage that they are good for you. Beans being the exception – they are good for the heart, as every schoolboy knows. The highest parp ratings on record, in my experience anyway, are scored by the humble onion bhaji. The parpsichord has been heard commencing its foul melodies whilst the onion bhaji is still being chewed, and on one memorable occasion before the onion bhaji has even been removed from its foil container. The only item more thoroughly parpicious than an onion bhaji would be a condom full of methane being carried across international borders by some sort of gaseous drug mule, which then splits in transit.

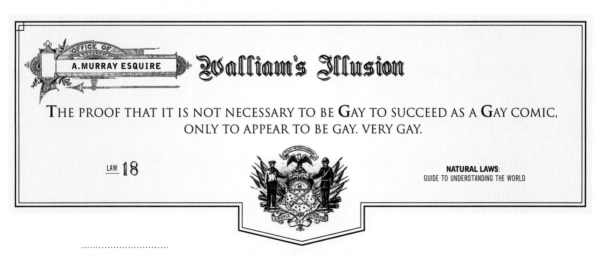

OFFICE OF A.MURRAY ESQUIRE   **Walliam's Illusion**

THE PROOF THAT IT IS NOT NECESSARY TO BE GAY TO SUCCEED AS A GAY COMIC, ONLY TO APPEAR TO BE GAY. VERY GAY.

LAW 18

NATURAL LAWS:
GUIDE TO UNDERSTANDING THE WORLD

....

[94] See Winks, above.

DISPENSING VELOCITY

Put simply: I am hungry. I want Food. When can I have it? This is one of the most important aspects of the World of Nutrition, and yet it is barely touched upon by so-called experts in the field, some of whom seem more interested, frankly, in rooting around in the toilet and drawing far-fetched conclusions from what they find there. I don't eat the heads of Lego men, it was just that one time, and I thought it was a particularly tough piece of sweetcorn. OK?

Now, if you are looking for a quick dispensing velocity, and who isn't, then my advice is to avoid any establishment with knives and forks on the tables. Knives and forks in a rack next to a carvery, this is infinitely preferable. For best results I recommend opting for somewhere where you are required to lean on a piping-hot glass counter under which pre-deep-fat-fried food is visibly sweating away waiting for you.

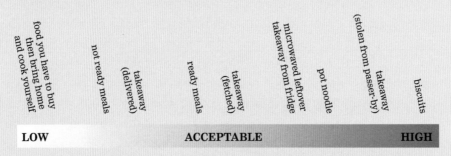

Fig 3. DISPENSING VELOCITY EXPLAIND

DATE BREATH

Some so-called experts would advise against eating before going out on a date, but I say it's not a bad idea. After all, if you arrive at a restaurant slightly full, there's less chance you will look like a pig when you've already finished your pudding while she is still picking brown bits out of the salad bar. You must always be aware, however, that what you put into your system will re-emerge during the evening in periodic gusts, and it is as well to make sure that these are as inoffensive as it is humanly possible to make them.

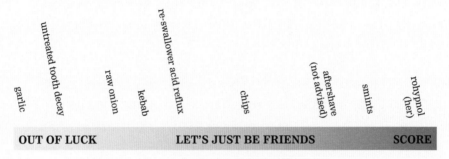

Fig 4. DATEBREATH EXPLAINED

BOOZE SOAKERS

A much under-rated aspect of Nutrition, but one that I think is worthy of serious consideration. A high booze soaker can help stave off a crippling hangover, aiding sleep by providing much-needed winks while going to work on soaking up the alcohol. It can help you avoid getting points on your licence by sitting stodgily on top of a mighty reservoir of beer, preventing it from gusting into the breathalyser. And, most importantly of all, it can provide the impetus and increased capacity for even more drinking.

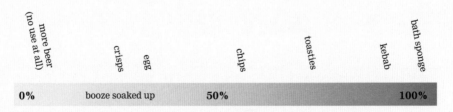

Fig 5. BOOZE SOAKERS EXPLAINED

This is another crucial aspect of the eating experience that is merely glossed over by the wafflers. How long will this meal take to make its way through the system? Have I got a better than fifty-fifty chance of making it home before the dreaded war-on-both-fronts commences? Or will I be asked to leave the bus?

Note: to collect more accurate data concerning your own digestive tract, try adding sweetcorn to a selection of foods, and then keeping a weather eye out for its re-emergence at what scientists refer to as the "other end". It is a very useful control substance, as it is both highly-coloured and therefore easy to spot, and it also remains remarkably unchanged by its transit through even the most acidic of environments. A word of caution, however. Adding sweetcorn to a cup of tea is not really worth the candle, and your statistics can be thrown out of whack by accidentally ingested Lego-man heads.

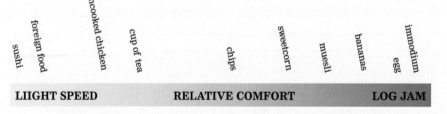

Fig 6. TURN AROUND TIME EXPLAINED

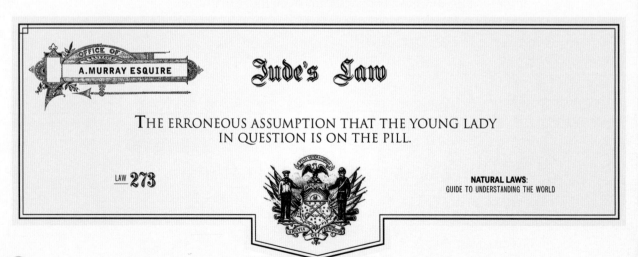

Here come the...

Fl⁰nsters!

The Plib
Farts when you tread on it.

8.3 Recipes

Did you know it's impossible to copyright a recipe? I laughed my head off when I found that out. That's why the Oliver boy does all that bish-bosh, pukka pukka stuff while he's going along, to disguise the fact that it's a Delia or an Ainsley or a Nigella he's reheating, the slobbering chancer.

And that's why I decided the time was right for me to release my own cookery book. Called *Cook Yourself British* by Al Murray the Pub Landlord, it is available now from all good bookshops[95].

Check out the next few pages for a bit of a taster (see what I did there?).

Jamie's favourite

[95] Where "good bookshops" are defined as "bookshops which stock COOK YOURSELF BRITISH by Al Murray the Pub Landlord".

COOK YOURSELF BRITISH

"The most exciting chef cook of our time" *Daily Yolk*

"Mr Ramsay eat your heart out... inspiring stuff" *The Egg Chronicle*

AL MURRAY

Welcome to my recipe book of Cook Yourself British.

I'm going to show you how to master the art of cooking great English food but with a simple British twist. None of that French fancy rubbish.

PREPARATION:

Before you begin, however, you will need to learn the art of cooking the humble fried egg. This is not as simple as it seems – patience is the key my apprentice. Follow the steps below carefully and you will be on your way to Great British food heaven in no time.

STEP 1:

Select your egg. Carefully now, this is serious business.

STEP 2:

Crack egg into frying pan. Don't worry about stray eggshell pieces, these can be the garnish.

STEP 3:

Cook egg over a medium heat for about 7–9 minutes until golden.

STEP 4:

After serving up on dish of choice, jovially chat to your friends bragging about how talented you are while the oil catches fire in the pan because you forgot to turn it off (see *Help yourself to Deal with Debt – Chapter 6.2*).

Omelette England 🏴󠁧󠁢󠁥󠁮󠁧󠁿

INGREDIENTS:

2 eggs

1 egg

lard

This is a tasty snack option that I don't make as much as I used to. It used to be my boy's favourite, that's why, and I haven't seen him for eight years, so thanks a lot for bringing that up. You insenstive bastards.

Anyway, what happened was this. Me and the boy were watching an England game on the telly. I don't know if he even supports England any more. My heart is an empty husk... I forget where his mother was at the time. She used to do an evening class, learning French, maybe that's where she was, I don't know. So we get a bit peckish, and it falls to me to rustle something up. I go to the fridge, grab a box of eggs, and start to whip up an omelette. He used to love an omelette. I don't know if he even eats omelettes any more... Sorry, distracted myself there. Anyway, the omelette gets to the point where you put stuff in it. Bit of cheese, maybe, or a bit of bacon, or some crisps.

I shout out to the boy: "What do you want in your omelette?"

He shouts back: "What have you got?"

I look in the fridge, and there's nothing in there, nothing at all. I go to the food cupboard, and there's nothing in there either. All I've got is a couple more eggs. Now obviously I could have nipped down to the end of the road and fetched some stuff, or even sent the boy to get something, but there was an England game on, so that wasn't an option. So I shout to him: "I've only got eggs." And he shouts back: "All right, I'll have a fried egg in it then." Well, I don't mind telling you that I've got a tear of pride trickling from either eye as I tell you this story. A fried egg in an omelette? Genius!

So I grab another frying pan, fry up an egg, and pop it into the omelette just as it's ready to be folded over. I pop it on a plate, and bring it through to where he's sitting, just as the game gets really exciting. Germany it was, and the ball comes over and Shearer scores just as I'm saying to the boy:

"Here's your omelette... ENGLAND!"

He tucks in, and England win the game but end up getting knocked out by Romania as per bloody usual. A couple of days later we're getting peckish again and he says to me: "Dad? Can we have that Omelette England again?"

Which is how the name stuck. In fact, shouting England after the name of any meal came to mean stick a fried egg on it. Chips England? Egg and chips. Egg and Chips England? Two eggs and chips. All Day Breakfast England? All Day Breakfast with an extra fried egg on it. You get the idea with that.

In case you didn't pick it up just now as we were going along, how you make Omelette England is this. Use the two eggs to make an omelette. Fry the one egg. Put it in the omelette. Da-naah! Omelette England.

WINKS:	17 (add 10 if with chips)
PARPS:	high to toxic
DV:	technically a not-ready meal
BREATH:	eggy
BOOZE SOAKER:	2 units
TURN AROUND:	a 3 egg log jam
CHOLESTEROL:	clogging

Welsh Rarebit England

INGREDIENTS:

1 cheese toastie

1 egg

lard

The Welsh are great pub eaters. For some reason they like to spend as much of the day as possible in darkened hovels. It reminds them of the days when there were pits and they all had jobs.

Now your Welsh Rarebit is a straightforward piece of kit that even your work experience trainee chef should be able to manage. It's melted cheddar cheese on top of some toast. You can mix it with other stuff if you like, if you feel a bit fancy. Bit of mustard, maybe, or some Worcestershire sauce, or even a bit of ale, make it into a bit of a sauce, pour it onto the toast. It's your funeral. However you put it together, though, it's basically just a bog ordinary cheese toastie. There I've said it.

What I don't understand is how this came to be called Welsh Rarebit. I mean, the 'rarebit' part of it is probably just the word rabbit pronounced in that sing-song accent they all have over there. Imagine this phrase in your head, for example, and you'll see what I mean:

"Hullo everybody, I'm Sir Tom Jones, and this is my pet rarebit Englebert Humperdinck..."[96]

Maybe, back in the old days when folk had a passion for arbitrarily naming stuff, someone in Wales had a cheese toastie that looked a bit like a rabbit – a rarebit, sorry Sir Tom – and it just sort of stuck. I don't know. You can't blame me, I wasn't there. Perhaps we're lucky that that same someone didn't get a toastie shaped like a flying saucer or the baby Jesus.

How did the Welsh get to be in charge of it, though? That's the bit that baffles me. Look at what it's made of. Cheddar cheese, from Cheddar in England (not Wales), Worcestershire sauce from Worcestershire in England (not Wales), mustard (English mustard, obviously, not Welsh), bread from... well, Sainsbury's I suppose (and I believe, in all fairness, that they do have one or two outlets in Wales, but really, come on...).

I think you would have to agree that it is nothing short of a travesty that the humble cheese toastie has been mystifyingly appropriated by the Welsh, and so in order to redress the balance I suggest you fry an egg in some lard, whack it on the top of your cheese toastie, and then tuck into your Welsh Rarebit England.

WINKS:	21 (add 10 if with chips)
PARPS:	tolerable to amusing
DV:	technically a not-ready meal
BREATH:	cheesy/eggy
BOOZE SOAKER:	1.5 units
TURN AROUND:	a 3 egg log jam
CHOLESTEROL:	some back up

[96] I believe he has two, the other one is called Cerys out of Catatonia.

Buck Rarebit England

INGREDIENTS:

1 cheese toastie

2 eggs

lard

water

There is a bastard variant of the (so-called self-styled) Welsh Rarebit (ie: the plain old honest to goodness cheese toastie), which is known as the Buck Rarebit. This, in some ways, could be seen as an historical precursor to the whole "whacking a fried egg onto the top of things and calling them something else" school of cuisine which I myself am currently promulgating[97]. What is involved is a cheese toastie, using the cheese of your choice – even Welsh cheese if you want to, although the Welsh themselves don't seem that keen on it, which can't be a good sign. Then you poach an egg – yes, you heard me right, you poach it – scoop it out of the pan as best you can with a spoon or possibly a small net of some kind and then plop it soggily onto the top of the toastie.

Now, any humble nutritionist such as I am myself will tell you that the poached egg is the fried egg's pale and weedy younger brother, cooked in warm water and so lacking all the essential health-giving goodness of the lard.

My recipe for Buck Rarebit England therefore evens up the nutritional balance, not by removing the poached egg, no, that would be wrong-headed and a farce. No, simply fry another egg in your lard, and pop it alongside the poached one. Thus all nutritional bases are covered in one tasty plateful[98].

WINKS:	25 (add 10 if with chips)
PARPS:	a two egg duet
DV:	technically a not-ready meal
BREATH:	cheesy/eggy
BOOZE SOAKER:	1.7 units
TURN AROUND:	stringy poached egg confuses intestines
CHOLESTEROL:	medium congestion

---

[97] Not sure about this word. If it means something to do with sex then just ignore it.
[98] You can leave the poached egg if you want.

Croque[99] Monsieur[100] England

INGREDIENTS:

1 ham & cheese
toastie

1 egg

lard

Now I'm sure you won't be surprised to discover that I don't have a great deal of time for French cooking. I don't have a great deal of time for the French full stop, their cooking even less so. I do, however, have a French dish in my repertoire[101], and I stumbled upon it completely by accident (honest) as follows.

One lunchtime in the pub this French bloke Jean François who was hanging around a lot at the time[102] asked for a ham and cheese toastie. This was around about the time when I had the work experience trainee chef on the strength (very keen, had his own knives), and he got a bit carried away. Put the cheese, if you can believe this, on the outside of the toastie! I mean, how simple can a recipe get? Shove cheese and ham between two bits of bread, and stick it in the toasted sandwich machine. A child of five could do it, and I should know as I have recently been employing one for that very purpose.

So anyway, the work experience trainee chef hands over this sorry-looking excuse for a toastie with a soppy grin on his face, and then goes back to scraping all the burnt cheese off the Breville with a cross-head Phillips screwdriver[103]. I can see the machine's going to be out of commission for a while, and anyway it's only Jean François so I can't be bothered to throw it away and make another one, so I popped a quarter[104] of a tomato on top of it and took it out to where he was sitting.

---

[99] French word. [100] French word. [101] French word.
[102] See MY MISERABLE LIFE by Al Murray the Pub Landlord.
[103] See How To Write Your Own Alan Bennett Play, THE PUB LANDLORD'S BOOK OF BRITISH COMMON SENSE by Al Murray the Pub Landlord.
[104] No need to go mad.

Well, I wasn't expecting him to be pleased, but he sat back and threw his hands in the air in amazement, which I thought was a bit much.

"Oh la la!" he cried, which I didn't know they really did in real life. "Oh, but this ees a crock, monsieur!"

Here we go, I thought, the bleating's begun, and I started explaining about the work experience trainee chef, and how it looked terrible but would probably taste all right, but he butted in and stopped me in mid-stride.

"Non, non, Gouv-eur-ornor!" he said, excitedly. "This is a Croque Monsieur, a traditional authentique French platteur. Just like Maman used to make!"

And blow me if he didn't wolf the whole mess down and ask for another, kissing his fingertips in the way the French do to indicate deliciousness.

So that was how I learnt a little bit of French cuisine. Croque Monsieur = a knackered-up ham and cheese toastie. I devised an extra twiddle of my own, which was to slap a fried egg on the top to create the Croque Monsieur England. Thought it might take the curse off it, you know.

I even ended up adding it to the blackboard for a while, but people kept making cracks about how I was going gastro and what have you, so I rubbed it out again.

WINKS:	22 (add 10 if with chips)
PARPS:	under control – just
DV:	technically a not-ready meal
BREATH:	cheesy/eggy/hammy – you won't really smell the ham unless it's past its sell-by date
BOOZE SOAKER:	1.5 units
TURN AROUND:	medium – binding power of egg counteracted by loosening quality of off-ham
CHOLESTEROL:	some light chest thumping

Croque[105] Madame[106] England

INGREDIENTS:

1 ham & cheese
toastie

2 eggs

lard

Shortly after the invention of the Croque Monsieur England, as detailed
above, Jean François came in again and decided to give it a go. When
I plonked it down in front of him, he threw his hands up in the air as
before, and cried out:

---

[105] French word.
[106] French word.

"Oh la la!"

Which to be honest I was trying to discourage, as it made the whole tone of the place rather too confusing.

"What's the matter now?" I said.

"Oh, but mon cher Gou-veur-ornor! You have brought to me a Croque Madame! My all time favourite French snaque!"

Whereupon he grabbed my head and kissed me on both cheeks. Well, one cheek anyway, I managed to stiff arm him back into his seat before he landed the second smoocher. The bad news, though, I gathered as he tucked in with embarrassing eagerness, was that the Croque Monsieur England which I had proudly unleashed upon an unsuspecting public, thanks to a combination of the accidental cack-handedness of my work experience trainee chef and my own inspirational nutritional genius, had already been invented by a French bloke, and was in point of fact called a Croque Madame.

Now you know me, I am seldom down-hearted[107]. A few hours of concentrated brainstorming over a restorative pint or six, and I came up with an entirely new recipe, namely the Croque Madame England, which is very like the Croque Madame (which is exactly like the Croque Monsieur England) except instead of one fried egg on top of a ham and cheese toastie it has two. Enjoy.

WINKS:	27 (add 10 if with chips)
PARPS:	freeform
DV:	technically a not-ready meal
BREATH:	cheesy/eggy/hammy
BOOZE SOAKER:	1.9 units
TURN AROUND:	medium to high – binding power of egg beginning to overwhelm loosening quality of off-ham
CHOLESTEROL:	even more

[107] Apart from during the periods covered in MY MISERABLE LIFE by Al Murray the Pub Landlord.

Note: Fans of the hit musical **Cabaret!** *may also especially enjoy the Croque Mesdames et Messieurs England, which has four fried eggs. Or even the Croque Mesdames et Messieurs Meine Damen und Herren Ladies und Gentlemen England which has twelve.*

WINKS:	38 (add 10 if with chips, although you will be asleep before you can finish)
PARPS:	orchestral
DV:	slow, unless you have twelve frying pans
BREATH:	even eggier than Cool Hand Luke
BOOZE SOAKER:	12 units
TURN AROUND:	two weeks – those eggs are never coming out of there
CHOLESTEROL:	alert, defcon 4, signal at danger, do not pass, trained medical staff on call

Four in a bed. It'd kill you

Chicken Tikka Masala England

INGREDIENTS:

1 chicken tikka masala
1 egg
lard

Did you know that Chicken Tikka Masala is in fact a British dish? I don't mean because India used to be part of the Empire, although it did, which makes lots of other curries into British dishes too. In fact, the old Taj Raja at the end of the road (or is it Raj Taja? It might be Raj Taja...) might as well call itself a British takeaway. It doesn't, but it might as well do.

Anyway, the Chicken Tikka Masala came about, apparently, because of British people out for a curry finding the straight Chicken Tikka a bit dry, not to mention bright fluorescent red, and asking the waiter for some gravy to cover it up. Brings a tear to your eye, doesn't it? So this waiter goes into the kitchen and he and the chef botch some gravy together with a tin of tomato soup and a couple of other bits and bobs (what the eye don't see the chef gets away with). The punters love it, and ask the waiter what it's called, and he says "Um... Chicken Tikka... Masala, yes that's it, Masala!" And thus the dish was born. Masala just means mixture, that's all. The guy was busking it. Give him a biscuit.

Then people started asking for it in other Indian restaurants, and there are now at least fourteen distinct recipes for it up and down the country. The one in Glasgow glows in the dark, apparently, which should hold them up there until electricity arrives. Best of all, Brits on holiday in India have started asking for their favourite curry, not realising that it's a British dish, and the Indian restaurants in India[108] are now putting it on their menus. It's an inspiring story, in a coals-to-Newcastle sort of a way.

---

[108] In India, Indian restaurants are just called restaurants.

To make your British Chicken Tikka Masala even more British, follow the steps below:

1. Go to the end of the road and get a takeaway Chicken Tikka Masala from the Taj Raja (possibly Raj Taja...). And some poppadoms. And one of those naan breads with raisins in it for pudding.
2. When you get back, fry the egg in the lard.
3. Put the egg on top of the Chicken Tikka Masala.
4. Enjoy your Chicken Tikka Masala England.

WINKS:	22 (add 10 if with rice)
PARPS:	for god's sake don't make me laugh
DV:	low (delivered), medium (fetched), high (stolen)
BREATH:	sub-continental
BOOZE SOAKER:	3 units (5 with naan bread)
TURN AROUND:	do not go on long walk
CHOLESTEROL:	seething

582

Fugu Enguran
((FOO-goo EN-goo-ran))

INGREDIENTS:

1 raw blowfish

sake

2 eggs

lard

Fugu is the Japanese name for certain species of puffer fish or blowfish, which, though considered great delicacies, contain a poison so toxic it can kill. It's so imperative that fugu be cleaned and prepared properly that entire books have been written on the subject. In commercial Japanese kitchens, where this fish is used in both Sashimi and Nabemono preparations, only qualified cooks may deal with fugu, having undertaken an apprenticeship of three years.

Fugu contains lethal amounts of the poison tetrodotoxin in the internal organs, especially the liver and ovaries, and also the skin. The poison, which is a sodium channel blocker, paralyzes the muscles while the victim remains fully conscious, eventually dying from asphyxiation. There is no known antidote. Some professional chefs prepare the fish so there is a minute amount of poison left in the meat, giving a prickling feeling and numbness on the tongue and the lips. The most popular dish is Fugu Sashimi, also called Fugu Sashi or Tessa, sliced so thin that the pattern of the plate can be seen through the meat. These plates are often decorated so that the removal of each slice will create an aesthetically pleasing effect. The fins of the fish are fried and served in hot sake, creating a dish called Fugu Hire-zake.

Invite a qualified Sashimi or Nabemono chef to your house to prepare the blowfish for you. When he is nearly finished, you fry the eggs with a knob of melted lard. Once the Fugu is prepared by your chef and laid out in the approved fashion – which it can take many years to master, remember, so don't rush him – put the fried eggs on top. Might be an idea to wait until he's not looking. Serve with chips and brown sauce.

NB: If you experience chest pains or left arm numbness after eating Fugu Enguran, this may be due to cholesterol overload rather than the blowfish poison.

WINKS:	-4 just thinking about the tetradotoxin will keep you awake (add 10 if with chips)
PARPS:	potentially lethal
DV:	really slow, unless sashimi chef is your flatmate
BREATH:	distinctly briny
BOOZE SOAKER:	0.7 units, a light and porous dish
TURN AROUND:	might want to eat while sitting on toilet – seconds count
CHOLESTEROL:	not your problem with this one

Pink Grapefruit Sorbet
England

INGREDIENTS:

369 g large pink or red grapefruit, scrubbed

200 g white sugar

60 ml light corn syrup

950 ml water

1 dash red food colouring (optional)

1 egg

lard

This is a well-known classic palate cleanser for a multi-course gourmet meal, but can also be a *Starter* or a *Pudding*.

1. Use a vegetable peeler or large zester to remove 3 long strips of peel (just the zest, not the pith) from the grapefruits. Set aside. Squeeze out 2 cups of grapefruit juice.

2. In a saucepan, combine the grapefruit peel, sugar, corn syrup and water. Bring to a boil, stirring to dissolve the sugar, and cook for about 2 minutes. Set aside to cool. Place in the refrigerator, or set in a bowl of ice for faster chilling. Discard the peel.

3. Strain the grapefruit juice through a sieve or strainer to remove the pulp. Discard pulp. Stir the sugar syrup into the grapefruit juice, and mix in food coloring one drop at a time to achieve a pleasing, believable pink. (In other words, don't overdo it.)

4. Pour into the container of an ice cream maker, and freeze according to the manufacturer's instructions. Transfer to a container and freeze until firm before serving.

5. Fry egg in lard and serve on top.

WINKS:	2 (may even be a negative number if juice squirts into your eye, or if hot egg fails to cancel out ice cream headache)
PARPS:	ordinary single-egg parpery
DV:	slow, a lot of faffing about, especially if you have to buy an ice cream machine before you can start)
BREATH:	zesty/eggy
BOOZE SOAKER:	0.001 units – no use at all, the whole idea of the dish is to leave room for something else
TURN AROUND:	moderate (mostly wee, actually)
CHOLESTEROL:	grapefruit nil, egg some

Essential

Steak and Kidney Pie
England

INGREDIENTS:

1 Fray Bentos Steak
and Kidney Pie

2 eggs

lard

A British Twist on an English classic

First take the lid off the Fray Bentos Steak and Kidney pie and stick it in the
oven (not the lid, stick that into the recycling). When it's nearly ready, fry the
eggs. Take the Fray Bentos Steak and Kidney pie out of the oven. Put the fried
eggs on the top. Serve.

WINKS:	24 (add 10 if with chips, although you will find there isn't really room in the tin for them)
PARPS:	two egg harmonics
DV:	another not-ready meal, but worth the wait
BREATH:	kiddly
BOOZE SOAKER:	4 units – that soggy puff pastry has plenty of capacity
TURN AROUND:	unexpected gristle can delay service
CHOLESTEROL:	teeming

Healthy Option England ✚

INGREDIENTS:

spinach

kale

rocket

iceberg lettuce

watercress

endive

red chard

oak leaf lettuce

artichoke

radicchio

little gem lettuce

1 egg

lard

Healthy Option England. You can leave the greenery if you want, it's mostly just garnish.

This is a really healthy option, with lots of greenery and goodness, and it'll probably bung you up for the best part of a fortnight. Get a big bowl, and tear up all the assorted leaves and stuff and put them in the bowl. Then toss them using some salad tossers – this is a kitchen implement, not a slang term for Jamie Oliver and Gordon Ramsay. Put this to one side while you fry your egg in the lard. Then put your fried egg on top of your leafy salad for your Healthy Option England[109].

WINKS:	8 (add 10 if with chips)
PARPS:	reedy
DV:	fast, only egg needs cooking, the rest is just tearing up leaves
BREATH:	depends on dressing – mint, Hugo Boss
BOOZE SOAKER:	1.2 units
TURN AROUND:	lot of roughage there, probably safe to embark on a medium-sized expedition of some kind
CHOLESTEROL:	salad is the natural enemy of cholesterol, so you may need to replace lost cholesterol with more eggs

Jellyfish England

(Inedible)

WINKS:	-20 (night terrors – add 10 if with chips)
PARPS:	parpsichord may break into Octopus's Garden
DV:	incredibly slow, once you've booked the flights, taken scuba diving lessons, hired local guides etc etc, and by then you've probably filled up on biscuits anyway
BREATH:	fishy, with dangling tendrils
BOOZE SOAKER:	2 units – the fish drinks one unit all by itself
TURN AROUND:	rapid, a real ring stinger[110]
CHOLESTEROL:	low (no egg)

[109] You can use the melted lard as a salad dressing.
[110] See Pacific Rim – Ring of Fire.

Here come the...

FlOnsters!

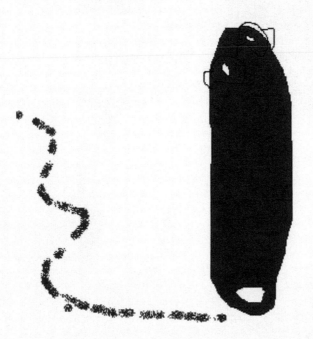

The Bookywook
Not as clever as it thinks it is.

CHUMP

⁓ FORREST GUMP ⁓

"Life is like a box of chocolates, you never know what you're going to get"

Forrest Gump is a film, so don't panic, I know it's not real. I know if someone's on the TV they're not real (apart from me when I do it). There was a time not so long ago, however, when everyone thought that this film was the absolute bee's knees and a fount of homespun true life actually helpful wisdom that you could use to Help Yourself.

It was a simple heartwarming simple tale of a simpleton whose simple way of doing things simply meant that he simply succeeded at whatever he put his simple mind to, thus proving that America thinks of itself as a simple heartwarming place where even total fucking idiots will be successful.

The chocolates line was the thing that everybody went on about, how deep it was, and how very very true. Forrest's mum (or rather, mom) said it, and everyone loved the way Forrest would repeat it in the droning voice of a moron, which paradoxically made it sound even more wise (see Gump Change). But of all the supposedly wise sayings that you run into this possibly is the most Unhelpful of the lot. Any self-respecting box of chocolates has a thing with pictures on telling you which ones are which, or the different chocolates are wrapped in wrappers that say what they are, like mini-Bountys, so it's actually really really difficult to be surprised by a box of chocolates. Now if he'd said:

"You never know what you're going to get in Life... Chocolate?"

that would have been a lot more Helpful. And you'd actually be being offered a chocolate (albeit by a stranger who's a moron on a bench), which you'd be able to identify using the helpful diagram provided, rather than a half-arsed and frankly Unhelpful pearl of nonsense. Although my old mum used to say: never accept sweets from a stranger who's a moron on a bench. Or go back to his house to look at puppies.

Case History #5

Name	Wordsworth
Age	20's
Sex	Male

Subject: A bloke who only turns up on quiz nights. There he is, look. Learning.

Description: Male, twenties, probably student. He has a long stripy scarf, anyway. And a gonk.

Problem: This youth would only show up when there was a quiz night on at the pub. Now, I've got no problem with that, that's what quiz nights are for, in a way, isn't it? To drag in a whole new stratum of clientèle[111], if you will. Trouble with this feller, though, is that he knows everything, it's impossible to catch him out. He must spend all afternoon watching *Going for Gold* and old *Fifteen to Ones* on The Quiz Channel, because that's where I get the questions from. Anyway, it was starting to get people down. Everybody wants a fair crack at winning the frozen chicken[112], after all, don't they? But when this bloke came in people would chuck their pencils in the air and give up. They couldn't even beat him by nipping into the bogs with the mobile and phoning a friend. Quiz night was in danger of becoming an utterly pointless exercise. I started throwing in really obscure left-field questions, like "Who is the Chancellor of the Exchequer?", and he was getting those too. It was when he got a hundred per cent on a round which included the question: "What is Barrie's pin number?", that we started to wonder if something was up. Lucky guess, he said, but Barrie never did get the benefit of all those subscription porn channels his bank statement claimed he was paying for. To make matters worse, this youth wasn't even drinking. He'd nurse a pint of tap water the whole evening, not contributing to the carvery fund in any way.

Solution: I threatened to bar him, but this feller was very clued up, and started spouting bye-laws and stuff at me about how I had a duty to admit him under the terms of my licence. Two can play that game, though, and a bloke I know down the Honourable Order[113] tipped me the wink that I could make "purchase of an alcoholic drink" one of the conditions of entering the quiz. Of course, this herbert whined that "he didn't like the taste of beer",[114] but after a couple of quiz nights he was hooked on alcopops and now he can barely remember his own name let alone the capital city of anywhere.

Prescription:

[111] French word.
[112] Including giblets.
[113] Of publicans.

Signed

Mind & Body

H A R M O N Y

Help Yourself to Wellness experts tell us that the way to holistic[114] health is through creating harmony between the Body and the Mind. What they mean is that when your Body feels a bit rough, your Mind should try to help out by buying their book on achieving Wellness through Mind/Body Harmony, but still, maybe they're onto something.

Are your Mind and Body in Harmony? These examples may help you work this out.

[114] I don't get it either.

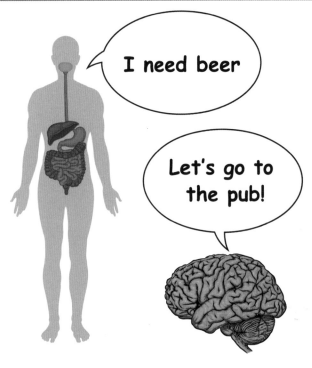

MIND-BODY HARMONY?

RESULT:

Wellness (also mild inebriation, followed by more serious inebriation, followed by Unwellness)

MIND-BODY HARMONY?

RESULT:

Unwellness (followed by pub-based conflagration)

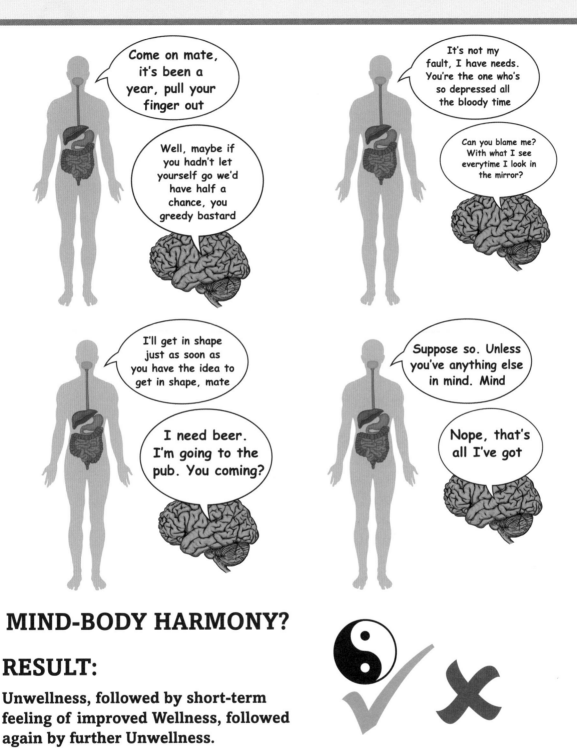

MIND-BODY HARMONY?

RESULT:

Unwellness, followed by short-term feeling of improved Wellness, followed again by further Unwellness.

Conclusion: The way to Mind-Body Harmony is to let the Body have its way. It's going to be all you have left in the long run in any case.

Help Yourself to Happiness

(Happiness: How to spot it if you've not come across it before that is.)

We all want to be happy. In fact there's those who say Happiness is the reason we were put on this Earth (and for most of us the reason we ended up on this earth is as a result of two drunken people's fumbling, transitory and ultimately drab groping for some fleeting hint of Happiness on the back seat of a second-hand mid-range saloon car).

Why then do so few people seem to be happy? Even in this, the greatest nation on the planet, you can't move for bitching, whingeing and bloody moaning. Surely this is something worth dissecting properly. Of course, Happiness could well be like a living creature, and the very act of trying to dissect it will kill it stone dead, like a rat in biology. But if that's something I have to do for you, my reader, I will. It is my solemn pledge and duty to you that I will kill Happiness if that turns out to be necessary (with a lethal injection is probably how I'll do it if I can get hold of one. I have got a claw hammer but that would be a bit messy and the animal rights lot might complain, even though we're not actually talking about killing an actual rat here, brains everywhere, it'd be great, I hate rats, who doesn't...? Where was I...?)

Like many of the big topics tackled in this book there's a whole bunch of myths about what Happiness is that need to be cleared up first of all if I'm going to do my job properly. Let's take a look at just a random handful of them:

happiness

MONE

love

9.1 Happiness: The Myths

1) Money can't buy you Happiness.
Oh come off it! Give me a load of cash
and I'll happily try and prove you
right. Just think how happy you'd be
just to be asked to *try* and prove that
money can't buy you Happiness. It'd
be fantastic! And by the way it can buy
you love too, or something that to all
intents and purposes resembles love
without all the other stuff like disputes
about housework, asking about her day,
explaining why you never came in last

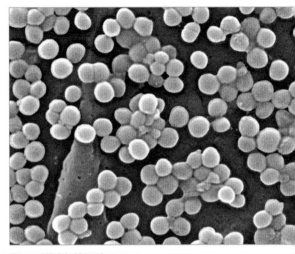

Fig. 1. MRSA. Nurse!

night, etc., the things that really take the edge off, you know. Money is
also credited with making the world go round, and I think this
is probably true, though the Science Lot would stick their
oar in and say it was gravity that makes the world go round,
but then it was money that paid for the research that helped
them find that out so they can shut up.

science
labs

**2) Happiness is contagious; if you are near it,
you will catch it.** The only thing I've caught
recently is MRSA after going into
hospital for an ingrowing
toenail. Broken Britain!

**3) Those who bring sunshine
into the lives of others, cannot keep it
from themselves**. The bloke who said this was called
J M Barrie and he wrote *Peter Pan*. Grow up.

**4) Happiness is not something you can hold in your
hands, it's something you carry in your heart.** That's as
may be, but you can still buy stuff to hold in your hands that
will make you pretty happy, (see point number 1, above). And

Go. Away.

190

there are other things you can imagine getting your hands on that would make you happy, and where offering to pay for the privilege might spoil the mood (see Liz Hurley).

5) Happiness is a cigar called Hamlet.
Not any more, mate, thanks to Health and Safety. You have to go out into the car park, whatever the weather, and smoke it like a desperate needy outcast, and who's that going to make happy? The only people who really thought this was true, even in the old days before lung cancer, were the "creative geniuses" who write adverts. "What men talk about down the pub!" please, spare me...

6) Independence is happiness. My wife and son left eight years ago, I'm so alone, thanks for bringing that up. And look at America, they achieved independence 200 years or so ago[115], and you're not going to tell me they're happy are you? The amount of misery eating that goes on over there? You have to admit the only reason they voted in a black president last year is because the white guy in charge had made them so desperate and miserable and universally loathed, they thought "might as well give it a go". It wasn't because they actually liked him. (Yeah, satire).

---

[115] Well, that's what we let them think.

7) Happiness is a warm gun. Actually to be fair, this is debatable; it really depends who you've just shot. If it's, say, ooh I don't know, your second best mate in a late night game of drunken strip Russian roulette whilst watching *The Deer Hunter*, you'd feel pretty mortified, believe me. However, if it was, say, the French bloke who ran off with your missus taking your boy with him, in the back of the leg whilst on a day trip to Calais in the car park of Hypermarket Carrefour, then this statement would be quite close to the mark. Just a shame it was an air rifle, as air rifles don't actually get that warm, and I'm not sure the pellet even penetrated his trousers. I dropped the second pellet when I had to break the gun

Fig. 2. Deer hunter

over my knee and he'd scarpered by the time I got the tin open and found another. Next time... Of course, the bloke who thought up this phrase was John Lennon, and clever clever blokes who find this fact ironical should probably bear in mind that he was singing about his tudger.

8) Happiness is just an illusion. Not an illusion like that ponce David Copperfield making the Empire State building disappear. Why were they so impressed by that? When someone did actually make New York landmarks disappear the Yanks weren't so impressed with the mystical illusions of Mr Osama Bin Laden, were they? Nor is it an illusion like the kind they do on the waterfront at Blackpool where the bloke fools you every time with the Ping-Pong ball the lying cheating Northern bastard! Proper fleeced I was. The patter was really good and the next thing I knew I was down £120, the lying cheeky Northern bastard[116]. So, no, Happiness is not an illusion, unless that is you look at it from the point of view of David Copperfield and the cheeky Northern bastard. I expect they had a whale of a time.

[116] The fact that he was Northern is included here to give you an illustration of what he was like, I am not saying that his being Northern has anything to do with his being a lying cheeky bastard, just a coincidence, ok? Though maybe if he'd been a Southerner I'd have been onto him sooner, but I was giving him the benefit of the doubt, ok?

Here come the...
Flonsters!

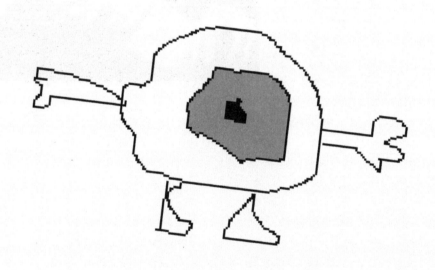

The Nerdbugler
It's an eye.

9.2 What Thinkers Think

There's no point thinking about Happiness too much as what you'll do is waste time you could otherwise use being happy. Unless, that is, you're the sort of person who finds Happiness in thinking about Happiness. Plato[117] for example, wasted so much time thinking he never ever managed to pull a bird, hence the word 'platonic', which means the relationship you have with a bird when you haven't managed to pull her. Imagine that, giving your name to Friday night failure. I bet he wasn't happy about that.

Benjamin Disraeli, a former Prime Minister of this great realm of ours, took the opposite view. He said: "Action may not always bring Happiness, but there is no Happiness without Action". He was a devil with a skinful on a Friday night, by all accounts.

The Christians[118], as always, have an all-encompassing, unselfish kind of theory on the matter. They say: "Happiness is Christianity". Genius, that's lunch lads. If only things were that simple, eh? Especially when all the Christians I meet are miserable gits who aren't allowed to watch porn. I'm not saying that that's Happiness, necessarily, but it certainly helps to stave off the misery for a few minutes. Where in the Bible is there any mention of porn at all? In fact, I'm not sure any of the major

www.thebibleboshers.com   *The Best Christian Porn Online!*

Error Reporting

404 Error!

404 Error - Not found

The file 'Virgin Mary' could not be downloaded for legal reasons

Cancel

Fig. 3. Not your typical virgin

---

[117] My favourite Greek philosopher has to be Mediocretes, the bloke who invented the average. He wasn't having a good day, he wasn't having a bad day, it wasn't the best idea, it wasn't the worst idea, but it was just about good enough.

[118] The two thousand-year-old religious movement, not the mob who did *Harvest For The World*.

religions mention porn, certainly not in the modern DVD or downloadable digital formats, so why have they got such a downer on it? And who wants to look at a mucky tapestry nowadays? No point in freeze-framing it, it's all one big freeze-frame. They didn't think that one through.

Fig. 4. Who looks happier to you?

Buddha[119] based his whole religion on Happiness and the pursuit thereof, and if you look at him he's just some big old fat bloke sitting round not doing much. They never portray him in sculpture putting out the bins or washing the car, he's always just sitting around on his backside doing nothing. So is that the answer? It's certainly more appealing from a lifestyle point of view than giving up the porn, isn't it? Buddha said that the best way to achieve Happiness was to avoid Misery (good luck with that) by avoiding Desire. In other words, don't get your hopes up, which is sound advice and also explains why he sat around doing nothing.

Your extreme sports types would take issue with old Buddha. It seems the more energy and effort they expend and the more danger they put themselves in the bigger the smiles get on their stupid faces. By the way, the term 'Extreme Sports' is a shortened version, and the full wording is '**Extreme**ly bloody stupid waste of time and tax payers' money when you clowns end up in A&E with a broken leg and by the way it's nothing to do

[119] I covered Buddha in the religion bit of the last book, and if any of this is different, it's because I've forgot what I wrote last time or I've changed my mind. Alcoholic licence.

with **Sports**'. There's no competitive element to bungee-jumping, so shut it, you Kiwi herberts. No one's impressed.

Look at your typical Extreme Sport pill and your Buddha side-by-side. Your Extreme Sportist is going to be a stringy sort, all muscle and sinew, isn't he, while your Buddha is, as we know, exceedingly plump due to his philosophy of complete inactivity. Which one has more Happiness? It's obvious, isn't it? Everyone knows fat blokes are more jolly. Just like everyone knows big girls are more bubbly and much easier to get on with than the pipe-cleaner types you try and chat up first on a Friday night[120].

A penis! a penis! The greatest gift that I possess!

More recently Ken Dodd, bless him – a man who you cannot imagine subscribing to the view that money can't bring you Happiness, otherwise he would hardly have so much of it stuffed under his bed in shoeboxes, would he? – opined that Happiness was the greatest gift that he possessed. For me it was a chopper bike that Uncle Barrie bought me. What a Christmas that was! My father was really cheesed off with Barrie for some reason, perhaps to do with the fact that he himself had only bought me a magnetic Travel Draughts set that he'd obviously picked up late on Christmas Eve at the petrol station. Good old Doddy brought us all the gift of laughter, didn't he? Especially when he sang that *Happiness* song, because it sounds like he's singing: "A penis, a penis, the greatest gift that I possess…"

---

[120] As my Dutch friend says, "the meat must shake".

9.3 Measuring Happiness

So what's Happiness and how can we spot it
in this day and age? How can you tell someone
is happy? Can you measure it? How long
is cheerful? Do the French have their own
arbitrary scale for measuring Happiness that
they're going to try to get us to use instead of
the perfectly good system that has served us for
centuries? Is Happiness measured in volume?
Or surface area – minutes happy x distance
travelled while happy? Not sure, frankly, but
what would probably be good is to try looking
for a few telltale signs of Happiness.

1.0 ||||||||||||||||||||||||||||||||||||||||||||||||||||||||||

Matters of the heart is a good place to start. One way to spot
if someone's happy is if they're talking about their partner. You
only ever talk about your partner at the beginning and the end
of your relationship. So if it's the beginning,
they're going to be elated at the joy of the
springtime feeling a new bond brings.
And if it's at the end, it's another form
of Happiness generated by an
overwhelming sense
of relief, tinged
with regret at
the loss of half
the stuff. The
rest of the time
they're together

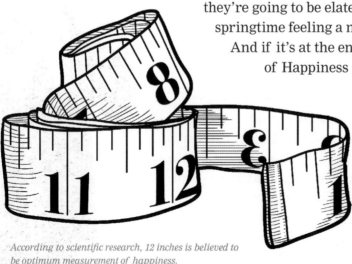

*According to scientific research, 12 inches is believed to
be optimum measurement of happiness.*

they don't say anything at all so the chances are they're not happy. Not unhappy, necessarily, just not happy.

2.0

If you talk to the nerds, they try to measure Happiness with something called the SWL Index or Satisfaction With Life index, where they look at quality of life, health, education, you know, all that nonsense. Now I've looked into this and as far I can see it all seems to be a total load of bollocks, as on the SWL World chart, Austria, Ireland and New Zealand are all above Great Britain. Broken Britain? Or a Broken Index? Actually I expect it's like Eurovision where all the pals get to vote for each other. No one likes us. We're too strong.

3.0

So if we can't tell people are happy it must mean that there's loads of people walking around being happy without us even knowing. So what's making them happy? Success[121]? It certainly isn't other people's Success. After all, other people's Success never makes you happy, unless you're married to them and reap the financial benefits and sometimes even that's not enough.

4.0

Talking to the lads – Steve, Steve, Alan and Steve – at the pub about Happiness, they feel it's derived from a great variety of things, ranging from a really great dump to finally getting that bogey you've been fingering for ages (Steve, in case you were wondering). And when I asked the one woman that's wandered into the pub in the last six months what Happiness would be for her, she said basically it would be getting rid of a bloke who only talks about having a crap and picking his nose (Steve, in case you were wondering. No, the other Steve. I think she quite liked Alan, but he wasn't interested).

---

[121] See *Success*.

BRAIN DEAD

～ TERRY HORNE & SIMON WOOTTON ～

Authors of a book called
Teach Yourself: Training Your Brain

These guys came up with a breakdown of what Happiness consists of, and gave it a handy, and rather appropriate[122], acronym, which is *BLISS*.
This is what it supposedly stands for:

B = Body Pleasures, **L** = Laughter, **I** = Involvement, **S** = Satisfaction, **S** = Sex

In fairness I should point out that they went into it a bit more thoroughly than that. *Body Pleasures*, for example, includes anything which gratifies the senses. In other words, scratchings (pork) for taste, smell and sight, scratchings (vinyl[123]) for listening, and scratchings (bollocks) for touch. *Laughter* and *Sex* are fairly self-explanatory and unsurprising, and also belong together in my experience[124]. *Involvement* means being totally absorbed in an activity, such that you are likely to say something along the lines of: "Doesn't time fly!" as you glue the four millionth matchstick onto your model of the *Queen Mary*. And *Satisfaction* consists of three elements, apparently. One is *Warmth*, the feeling that one is loved, or belongs. The second is *Appreciation*, the knowledge that other people applaud what you are and what you do, and reward you well for it. And the third is *Possession*, the enjoyment of being able to say: "This is mine!". You might very well feel that these causes of Happiness deserve to be separate categories all of their own rather than being lumped together under *Satisfaction*, but then the acronym would have had to be **BLIWAPS**, and I've a feeling that would have made Messrs Horne and Wootton themselves significantly less Happy.

Now, looking at this, am I the only one who finds himself plagued with the mental picture of a giggling idiot playing with himself with grim concentration in a public place while other people stand around clapping and throwing coins?

I have my own suggestion for Messrs Horne and Wootton and their acronym:

B = Beer, **L** = Lager, **I** = International[125] Beers, **S** = Stout, **S** = Shorts

May not make you Happy, but might just help you stave off the abject misery until the morning. You can substitute Stout and Shorts with Scotch and Sambuca without undermining the basic principle.

---

[122]I bet they were happy when they came up with this. [123]Not Duran Duran, unless you are trying to drive a recalcitrant Central American dictator from his compound screaming for mercy. [124]Hacking, mocking laughter, and very little sex. [125]Like that Berschlisselhimmler, Beer of the Black Forest, that the brewery keeps lumping on me.

9.4   *The Gift of Laughter*

We all like a good laugh, don't we?
Laughter makes us happy. *Of course it does.*

SLAPSTICK

Or does it? Do we not have to be happy first in order for the
laughter to begin? Laughter is, after all, the outward sign of
Happiness. You see a bloke laughing and you think he looks happy.
So we laugh when we're happy, not the other way round.

No, laughter doesn't make us happy, or we'd all spend the whole
time tickling one another and nothing would get done. So being
happy makes us laugh, that must be it. Although we can be down
in the dumps, can't we, and see something that really makes us
laugh, like for instance the dartboard falls on Gary's head while
he's bending down to pick his darts off the floor (he's really bloody
terrible at darts, Gary), but Steve doesn't notice 'cos he's dropped his
glasses into the urinal and is waiting for them to be disinfected, so
he throws anyway and sticks a dart right in Gary's arse (outer ring,

that scores 25). Then by the time you've stopped laughing at that you've really cheered up, haven't you? So has the sight of Gary in pain made you happy, and so you've laughed, or has it made you laugh, thus leading to Happiness? Bit of both, probably.

So Happiness makes us laugh, and laughter makes us happy. Thank Christ we got that sorted out. I was going a bit mental there for a minute.

So what makes us laugh? Jerry Lewis once said: "There are only seven jokes known to man." He then went on to suggest that five of them involved putting in funny false teeth and going cross-eyed, so he wasn't all that much help. My extensive researches have revealed, however, that humour comes from the following things, apparently:

- ★ **Recognition** — *It's Tommy Cooper!*

- ★ **The Unexpected** — *It's Henry Cooper!*

- ★ **The Surreal** — *It's a Mini Cooper!*

- ★ **Slapstick** — *Tommy Cooper's been hit by a Mini Cooper!*

- ★ **Double Entendre** — *A woman goes into a bar and asks for a Double Entendre, so the barman gives her one!*

- ★ **Misunderstanding** — *I don't get it!*

- ★ **Wordplay** — *Russ Abbott pretending to be Tommy Cooper dressed as Superman, except his name is Cooperman!*

I like Tommy Cooper. They'll never replace the old stars, will they? He's in three of my eight non-porn DVDs, and frankly I think even the *Die Hard*s would have been better with Tommy in them. "Heh heh heh, just like that, m**********r! Helicopter, building, building, helicopter..."

It would be nice, though, wouldn't it, to have some new stuff to laugh at? And that's why I have put together the following, to open up a whole new area of mirth that has been hitherto inaccessible.

Here come the...

Fl0nsters!

The Grimplebladder
Like, piss comes out of it all the
time, like, pissing helplessly, non-stop, until it gets empty,
then you have to fill it up with the funnel. Hilarious.

9.5 Help Yourself to Understand American Comedy

Laughter is the balm that eases the troubled soul. And in these tricky times those heroic toilers at the gag front are working night and day to provide entertainment to put a smile on our faces, and God bless'em for that. Hats off to Sir David Jason and Nicholas Lyndhurst, a courteous bow to Dawn French and Jennifer Saunders, and a casual doff in the direction of Robert Lindsay and Kris Marshall.

There comes a point, though – sad but true – when you've seen every single episode of *Only Fools And Horses* at least seven or eight times, when *The Vicar of Dibley* and *AbFab* are cranking out for the umpteenth time, and when you start to think that if you see another bloody episode of *My Family* you're going to go down to Television House and start wreaking havoc with your bare hands. And when that moment of crisis comes, it would be nice, wouldn't it, to be able to watch a bit of comedy from across the pond, just for a change?

Trouble is, though, they make it so bloody hard. It seems that American comedians are obliged by some sort of law to make jokes about something called a Twinkie at least five or six times in the course of any programme, which would be

"American Comedy Helpline. Frasier speaking"

fine if (a) we knew what the hell a Twinkie was, and (b) if the jokes were any good. They might be good, I have no way of knowing.

So, having identified the problem, I have come up with a solution. Whether you can be arsed to follow through on it is really up to you. But how long are you going to pay for the Paramount Comedy channel just to keep on flicking past it night after night looking for porn?

I have come up with an infallible system for understanding what Americans are going on about in their comedy shows, involving a straightforward insertion of proper references that we will all get. I'm happy to go down Television House myself and dub all these corrections into the American comedy shows myself, if that's what it takes to get *My Family* off the air. I can do the voices, don't worry. Failing that you can train yourself, using the handy checklist below, so that when you hear the American term you can have the appropriate reference on the tip of your tongue, ready to shout it at the screen instantly and impress (or annoy, depending on what they're like) your friends and family.

OFFICE OF A. MURRAY ESQUIRE

Boyle's law

Ref: BGT-09

THE LAW STATING THAT THE PLACING OF ENDLESS PRESSURE UPON AN UNPREPARED VESSEL WILL CAUSE SAID VESSEL TO CRACK/ACT STRANGE/END UP IN THE PRIORY.

NATURAL **12** LAW

NATURAL LAWS: GUIDE TO UNDERSTANDING THE WORLD

Fig. 5. Tasty

Your handy American comedy checklist starts here:

Twinkie *n* – a small spongy sweet bar, about the size of an individual swiss roll. It comes in a packet of one, though, so it's not like the individual swiss rolls we have over here that you get in packets of six at the supermarket. Nonetheless it's like a sort of swiss roll, except not rolled up at all. Like a sponge cake, shaped like a swiss roll, that's what I'm getting at. It has cream in the middle, which is vanilla flavoured. It used to be banana-flavoured, apparently, until the Great Banana Shortage of World War II. So Hitler is to blame... wait, not Hitler, the other feller, Tojo... see, it's a minefield the whole cultural reference thing[126]. Another thing is they're meant to last forever, and still be edible after nuclear holocausts, that sort of thing. And it's a slang term for a gay bloke, something to do with the way the cream spurts out, don't particularly want to think about that... (never confused).

Source text

 So when you hear an American comedy character say TWINKIE

Translated text

 You shout: INDIVIDUAL CREAM-FILLED SWISS-ROLL-STYLE CAKE

Note: You could also try shouting "Snickers!" – it's shorter, and sounds a bit like knickers, and consequently the sort of thing that, say, Kenneth Connor might have enjoyed shouting. It is an American word, though, anyway, so if they meant Snickers they'd probably just say "Snickers".

----

[126] See Tojo.

Tojo[127] *n* – the Japanese Prime Minister during World War II. Not quite the same as Hitler, in as much as he had an Emperor to answer to while Hitler pretty much made all the decisions for his team, but Tojo seems to be the one who's carrying the can for the whole taking-on-the-Americans fiasco. When Japan surrendered he shot himself, but also unlike Hitler, he missed himself. Was very apologetic about that.

Source text

So when you hear an American comedy character say TOJO

Translated text

You shout: HITLER

Note: A word of caution about just shouting "Hitler!" randomly whilst watching something in civilised company. Your companions may not have heard the reference you are correcting and so it may not be an advisable or appropriate thing to do[128]. *Of course, if you're watching a Mel Gibson film it may just work anyway.*

The Olsen Twins *n, pl* – these two, whose names are Mary-Kate Olsen and Ashley Olsen, are twins. They first appeared in American comedies when they were babies, taking it in turns to play the same baby character in a programme called *Full House*. This show ran for eight years in America, which means that everyone knows all about it over there. Now that the Olsen twins are in their early twenties, and

Everyone loves twins

[127] Yes, that's right, Tojo.
[128] cf Jon Gaunt's career-ending blurtation on talkSPORT radio, 2008.

are always out and about opening fashion chains or dating film stars, they are known for being eye-catching eye-candy. When they turn up in a joke, it will usually be as part of a sex fantasy about doing the dirty with a pair of really young good-looking twins...

Source text

 So when you hear an American comedy character say THE OLSEN GIRLS

Translated text

 You shout: THE CHEEKY GIRLS

Note: Granted the Cheeky Girls haven't been going out with any film stars as far as I know. One of them (Left Cheeky) was engaged to twisty-faced humour-free Lib Dem spokesbeing Lembit Opik for a while, until even she noticed that that was a poor idea. They're from Transylvania, and consequently not as clean cut as The Olsen Twins and a little more scary, especially if their Mum's in tow, but you wouldn't kick 'em out of bed, would you? I wouldn't anyway – it's been a year...

Gilligan's Island *n* – is the big one. Everyone in America used to watch *Gilligan's Island* when they were growing up, and can't help going on about it the whole time. It's like a sort of TV nostalgia Tourette's Syndrome. It has been proven[129] that it is impossible to watch a whole episode of American television without there being a reference to *Gilligan's Island* in it somewhere. It was a stupid show, apparently, in

....

[129] By scientists.

which the characters were all far-fetched, the sets were all shoddy and cheap, and the plots didn't really make sense.

Source text

So when you hear an American comedy character say GILLIGAN'S ISLAND

Translated text

You shout: BLAKE'S SEVEN

Note: There is an aspect of Gilligan's Island *to bear in mind, which is that they made a joke on the show of never saying Gilligan's first name. Blake off of* Blake's Seven *had a first name, which was 'Roj'. Beautiful futuristic British name. So if that's what the joke is in your American comedy of choice, you might want to substitute Morse when you're shouting. I mean Inspector Morse, obviously, not that you should just shout a lot of dots and dashes. You don't want people to think you're a nutter.*

....

Oreos *n, pl* – are like a bourbon biscuit, except larger, and round, and with white stuff in the middle so as to give the comedy yanks another opportunity for a piece of obscure gay slang. So it's two round chocolate biscuits, joined together with a crème filling (not cream, crème. Like the eggs). When Americans say 'cookies', this is usually what they mean. There is supposed to be a proper way to eat them, by separating the twin parts to lick out the crème (not cream) from inside, but that may be some sort of gay sex slang too. I don't know. I'm not really up with that[130].

....
[130] I think Alan Carr has a book out, though.

Source text

 So when you hear an American comedy character say OREOS

Translated text

You shout: BIG ROUND BOURBONS

Note: Oreos are spectacularly successful in America, so if you hear the phrase "she's the heiress to the Oreos fortune", that means "she is very very rich indeed".

To go on Leno *vi* – to appear on America's top chat show, which is actually called *The Tonight Show*. Jay Leno is the name of the host, a much-loved comic with a big chin, and the show is a national institution of sorts, so I dare say that if you ask Michael Parkinson he'd say the equivalent would be 'to go on Parky', adding that he once interviewed Muhammad Ali. Twice. However, *The Tonight Show* is on every day, which is difficult in our country on account of the more limited plugging celebrity pool. Parky never dared do it.

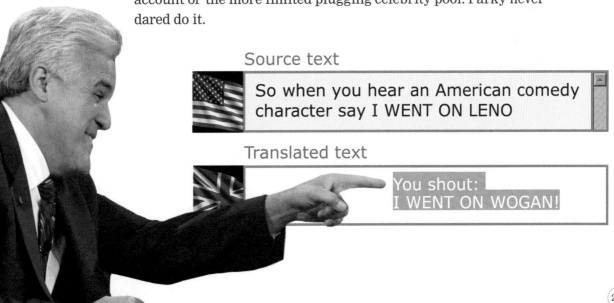

Source text

So when you hear an American comedy character say I WENT ON LENO

Translated text

You shout:
I WENT ON WOGAN!

Note: Unless the sense of the reference in question is "to urinate" rather than "to appear on chat show", in which case feel free to use Parky. David Letterman is the other chat show host in America who is often referenced in comedy shows and so on. His show is more like Jonathan Ross's, which happened because Jonathan Ross nicked it all off him. Apart from the Four Puffs and a Piano. Those are all Jonathan Ross's own idea.

....

Regis and Kathie Lee *n, pl* – the daytime chatshow hosts, who will have anyone on their show to plug anything. They've been on so long that no one even remembers their surnames (Kathie Lee has two first names, like one of the Olsen twins – see how good I am at this now?), and so, with due deference to Phil Schofield – Schofers, the old silver fox – and Fern Britton, his (ex)co-host on *This Morning* when it's not Mr and Mrs Eamonn, there remains only one real historical equivalent to this venerable pair of operators.

Source text

So when you hear an American comedy character say REGIS AND KATHIE LEE

Translated text

You shout: RICHARD AND JUDY

Note: For example, Kramer off of Seinfeld *went on Regis and Kathie Lee, played by themselves, to publicise his coffee table book which was also a coffee table. It was difficult for a British audience member (ie, myself) to appreciate this scene properly, not knowing who these people were or who they were supposed to be, and it only really came to life when Kramer vomited all over them.*

....

Bob Saget *n* – see The Olsen Twins, above. Not the bit about the sex fantasy, the other bit. He was the Dad in *Full House*, the spectacularly well-known American sitcom, in which he was the father of the Olsen Twins. He's done other stuff too, like presenting *America's Home Videos* for years and years, so he kind of has a reputation for always being on the telly and being prepared to do absolutely everything in a pedestrian light comedy way. A while ago. If they had made *Full House* in this country, then they'd almost certainly have used our favourite do-absolutely-everything light comedy actor.

Source text

 So when you hear an American comedy character say BOB SAGET

Translated text

 You shout: MARTIN CLUNES

Note: Bob Saget wasn't supposed to be all that good, and occasionally you will hear characters who are playing "actors" (in one of the many many hundreds of shows-about-shows) being afraid of being replaced by him, as though that would be a degrading and nightmarish development. In this context shout Neil Morrissey.

You again

Douchebag *n* – a common term of abuse in American comedy, as in the phrase "he's a real douchebag!" or "look out, here comes President Douchebag!". It doesn't sound like it's going to refer to anything nice, does it, and by God it doesn't, believe me. You know what an enema is, right? Where a tube is shoved up your jacksie in order to squirt water up where the sun don't shine? If you're a celebrity, apparently, in a posh health spa you can get it done with coffee for some reason, although why you'd allow anyone to force a liquid at pretty near to boiling point up there I can't imagine, let alone pay them to do it. (*Lots of milk in it for me, please, doctor...*) Now women, not to put too fine a point on it, have more than one – ahem – option when it comes to this particular genre of treatment. Think about it. I don't want to have to draw a picture[131]. And the container from which the warm water – or, as it may be, coffee – begins its awful journey is called the douchebag. You learn something every day.

Source text

So when you hear an American comedy character say DOUCHEBAG

Translated text

You shout: FRONT-LOADING LADY ENEMA EQUIPMENT

Note: *Interestingly, in olde Englishe comedy the enema was officially ranked as the funniest thing to refer to in the whole world(e), with senna pods and camp homosexuality also on the podium. You wouldn't want a coffee enema, though, would you, no matter how funny it was or how famous you got? Still, we've all seen the adverts – "we use the same high quality arabica beans for our decaffein- ated coffee as we do for the coffee we squirt up celebrities' rectums..."*

Cleanliness is next to Godliness

[131] Or copy one off the wall of the bogs.

The Superbowl *n* – a sporting contest between the two top teams in American Football, which is not really football at all, but a pastime for fat blokes who are too cowardly to play rugby. In fact, it's a bit like rugby if Health and Safety ever got hold of it. Crash helmets, shoulder pads, knee pads, shin pads, arse padding, chest protectors, groin protectors – they might as well drive around in armoured cars. And play keeps stopping every few seconds because one of them has fallen over and simply can't get back on his feet because of the sheer weight of his protective equipment, so everyone twiddles their thumbs while the buffoon is stretchered off on a reinforced wagon to a nearby crane to be righted. Even the Americans who are supposed to understand what's going on find it so excruciatingly dull that all they can talk about is what happens in the advert breaks. True. You remember that time a few years back when Janet Jackson's boob popped out during a dance routine? That happened during the interval in a Superbowl, and it's the

Source text

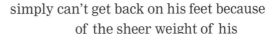

So when you hear an American comedy character say THE SUPERBOWL

Translated text

You shout: CUP FINAL

only thing anyone remembers about it. You ask any American Football fan whether they can remember the result, or even which teams were playing, and they'll be stumped. In truth it's all about cheese-covered nachos[132] to them. And it's in a different venue every year, instead of doing things properly at Wembley with Her Majesty in attendance (or failing that the Duke of Kent).

Note: Do not confuse this with a venue for ten pin bowling (also not a proper sport, by the way). There's a self-styled Superbowl out on the ring road, packed with fruit machines and video games, and somehow it has managed to get itself a licence to sell alcoholic beverages, which has made the representatives of the Honourable Order[133] very twitchy. All those teenage kids attracted to a life of alcoholic over-indulgence by all the flashing lights and loud noises, it's a disgrace. That's supposed to be our job.

....

Poindexter *n* – a term I have often heard bandied about in American comedy, and have never been able to work out whether it's a good thing or not. Well, turns out it comes from the old cartoon *Felix The Cat* from the olden days, about a cat (called Felix) who has a magic bag. There's a Professor, who wants the bag, but can't ever get his hands on it with hilarious consequences, and this Prof has a nephew called Poindexter who is frighteningly clever but also a bit

Source text

So when you hear an American comedy character say POINTDEXTER

Translated text

You shout: PENFOLD

....

[132] Tex-Mex. From Tex-Mexico.
[133] Of publicans.

of a nerd. So Poindexter is a nerd, a nerdy sidekick, in a cartoon. The nearest equivalent I can think of is that speccy verminous creature who used to hang around with Dangermouse in that cartoon, I forget the name of it[134].

Note: Alternative nerdy sidekicks include Syd Little (not a cartoon), Gromit (also not a cartoon, and not all that nerdy) and Justin Lee Collins.

So there you have it. A whole new world of America-based entertainment is now open to you, and about eighteen of the satellite channels will now start to make sense for the first time. If only I could get the hang of American Football – but that might just be a book too far for me[135].

[134] Dangermouse (Ed)
[135] See AMERICAN FOOTBALL EXPLAINED by Al Murray the Pub Landlord, as told to Sir Tim Rice, due for publication 2010.

Here come the...

Fl^onsters!

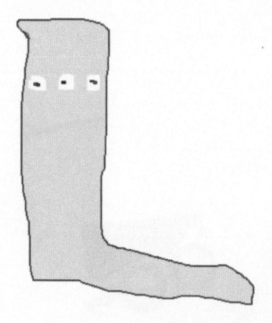

The Leg
Cos it looks like a leg.

9.6 Golden Rules

These are here for your simple perusal. They're the rules any sane person might live by. There are ten of them, but they're not for men in particular, so I'm not going to do anything so lame as call them the "Men Commandments" and box myself into a lousy concept.

The traditional Golden Rule from history is basically: "Love Your Neighbour as You Love Yourself". Jesus is the headline guy for that one, he gets all the credit and rightly so, he was British, but it's actually as old as the hills. By "neighbour" he meant everyone, not just the bloke next door, so he wasn't giving the green light to the idea of smashing the lights of the bloke two doors up's car because he parked in my space. Here's a load of versions off of the internet.

> "Do not to your neighbour what you would take ill from him." (*Pittacus*)
>
> "Avoid doing what you would blame others for doing." (*Thales*)
>
> "What you wish your neighbours to be to you, such be also to them." (*Sextus the Pythagorean*)
>
> "Do not do to others what would anger you if done to you by others." (*Isocrates*)
>
> "What thou avoidest suffering thyself seek not to impose on others." (*Epictetus*)

What a po-faced bunch of sandal wearing bastards[136].

But the basic problem of "Love Your Neighbour As You Love Yourself" is it comes from a time before stereos and illegal Chinese fireworks. Because of this basic Bronze Age shortcoming I have taken it on myself to come up with ten Golden Rules that will help you out in the immediate.

---

[136] "Do unto others as you would have others do unto you" is clearly the rule that those gay-fella-blokes follow, but they've got the wrong end of the stick, so to speak.

GOLDEN RULES

GOLDEN RULE 1:

Never be too keen. Being too keen is just going to make things worse for everyone, and may well Ruin It For Everyone Else.

GOLDEN RULE 2:

If you're going to make excuses, keep them brief. Everyone knows you're lying, the more stuff you add onto a lie the more likely it is you're going to get caught – and everyone else is lying too.

GOLDEN RULE 3:

Whatever it is, keep it to yourself, especially if it's an excuse that is beginning to wear thin because you went on about it too much and as a result left yourself open to Golden Rule 4 which is:

GOLDEN RULE 4:

Don't Get Caught (obvious really).

GOLDEN RULE 5:

If you've got nothing nice to say, say nothing, or better than that, say something nice. Don't say nothing nice.

GOLDEN RULE 6:

Putting yourself in the place of another, like Buddha suggests, means stealing someone else's place at the bar. That's why Buddha's so fat, he's been sat on your stool drinking your pint and eating your crisps. Don't do that, if ever there was a proper Golden Rule Number One that's it, but it's Number Six; nice one Buddha you donut.

GOLDEN RULE 7:

Don't get your hopes up. This is discussed at length in the Success bit of the book. If any of these rules is worth observing it's this one. With your hopes down you'll never be disappointed, which is the closest you can get to happy with any degree of certainty.

GOLDEN RULE 8:

Bear grudges. When the cold winter nights draw in and the feeling in your extremities starts to go, you'll regret not having any grudges to get your blood pumping – hang onto them, they could save your life – after all if it wasn't for the French and all that has passed between us we wouldn't know who we were (and they wouldn't know who they are either).

GOLDEN RULE 9:

If you can't sing, don't sing, and if you can't sing certainly don't sing and then ask if you can sing, thus forcing other people into having to make excuses which drives them in turn into breaking Gold Rule Number 2 (and be honest now, you know if you can't sing).

GOLDEN RULE 10:

"Love Your Neighbour As You Love Yourself" – yes, I know I said this didn't count anymore, but it's been difficult to come up with ten so I've fallen back on it. What it *really* means – and Jesus knew this, he was born in a pub – is get your round in.

QUANTUM

∼ DEEPAK CHOPRA ∼

Knock it off

Deepak Chopra is one of the world's leading Help Yourself experts, and has shifted more books than I've had Ploughman's lunches. Unlike a lot of the others, he's actually a doctor, so there's a real possibility he might be able to help you Help Yourself, if you're prepared to sit in his highly contagious waiting room with all the workshy skivers trying to get signed off for a couple of days. Oddly, though, his books aren't full of stuff like: "take some paracetamol and drink loads of fluids in the event of a cold," they're full of stuff that is meant to clear up the very mysteries of existence, etc.

He's in tune with the Universe, is Deepak, and he sees things on a Quantum[137] level. As well as hoping against hope that the next leap will be the leap home, he has said all sorts of wise things that maybe you could Help Yourself with (or to). Here's one:

"If you want to reach a state of bliss, then go beyond your ego and the internal dialogue. Make a decision to relinquish the need to control, the need to be approved, and the need to judge."

Just have a couple of pints and stop worrying about things for half an hour, Deepak mate. That'll take care of your control and your judgement, and you won't give a monkey's whether anyone approves of you any more. Then get a mini-cab.

[137]"Quantum" is a classic "shut up, you wouldn't understand" word. Anyone using it wants you to not ask questions and let them get on with knowing better than you.

Here come the...

Flonsters!

The Bloob[*]
Lives in a tree. Easy money.

*Don't use this name, it might have already gone.

DODGER ROGERS

Jack "Dodger" Rogers was the least reliable man in B Company.

Whenever action beckoned, "Dodger" would dive for cover!

His excuses were endless...

Sorry Sarge, I think I'm coming down with a cold

And...

Oh I don't know Sarge, I've got a rash

As well as...

I'm looking for volunteers for a very special mission

Nah, not interested

Hey! Has anyone seen my watch?

But come May 1940 even Dodger couldn't dodge the German Blitzkrieg! Hitler's Panzer armies swept into France and the Lowlands and pretty soon, B company were in trouble!

Right chaps, we're going to have to hold on if we're going to teach Jerry a lesson!

You can count me out, mate

The German attack was ferocious...

Die Englisher pig dog!!!

RAT-TAT-TAT-RAT

AIEEEEEEEEE.........!

Dodger did what dodgers do best – dodged!

This looks good!

Pretty soon this prize rat had company!

Shhh!! Keep it down lads!!

Eek!

Pretty soon B Company were in trouble!

The lads are getting slaughtered out there – better lie low!

RAT-TAT-TAT-RAT

AIEEEEEEEEE.......!

The German advance took them past Dodger's hidey hole and before he knew it, he was behind enemy lines

Lummel!

Then, Dodger saw a sight that made his blood run cold

Achtung, Spitfeuer!

TA TAT TAT

Blimey, it's Adolf!

Hmm....with my trusty rifle, I could bring the war to an end right now, sparing millions of lives and save the world from... ooh, I don't know – maybe five more years of hostilities

KILL THE BRITISHER PIG DOGS!

CLICK

CLICK

Nah, they might find out where I am

The battle raged ferociously all afternoon

Then, the sound Dodger was dreading...footsteps on the stairs outside

The door creaked open...

...and all of a sudden Dodger had company

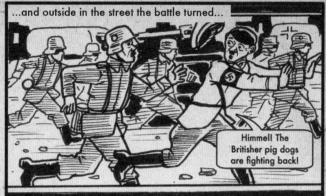

...and outside in the street the battle turned...

Himmel! The Britisher pig dogs are fighting back!

...as British reinforcements arrived

KA-BOOM!

RAT-TAT-TAT-TAT

AIEEEEEEE!...

We have retaken the town, but at what cost? All of B Company, wiped out!

Not quite all, Sir!

Good Lord, there's one man left standing!

He's a blooming hero!

Yeah, and I got a prisoner too. Hande Hoch, Fritz

The End

Case History #6

Name	Tina
Age	Mid 20's
Sex	Female

Subject: Just look at the photograph

Description: Australian barmaid. Fit[138].

Problem: As all publicans know, there's no better bar staff than your Aussie. They are genetically engineered for bar work, equipped to deal with any eventuality. I dare say you probably think that's nonsense, but bar work involves a highly specialised skill set, and not all nationalities are capable of it. You can't have Welsh bar staff in a public house that has a carvery, for example. They just help themselves to the beef.

When Tina came to work at my gaff (in response to my advert in the Honourable Order[139]'s monthly newsletter, specifying 'Fit Aussie Barmaid required for long hours in squalid grief hole. No timewasters or chancers') she was an immediate success. The regulars loved her easy-going antipodean demeanour, both of them, and she charmingly batted away their clumsy attempts to woo her with their leaden requests for jugs. I was so pleased with her work that I let her do longer hours so she could earn as much as she would have if she was a bloke. People got to hear about my great new Aussie barmaid, and new punters turned up every night, and came back the next night, and in short I'd never had it so good.

So what was the problem, I hear you ask? Well one fine day she decides she wants some legitimate employment paperwork doing, bit unusual for a member of the cash-in-hand economy, but I thought, since it was Tina, I'd be prepared to make an exception. So she brought her passport in. Turned out she was from Auckland, and not an Aussie barmaid at all. She was a Kiwi, and no one in their right mind would hire one of them to work in a pub. Not unless they want the whole place stuffed with dwarves and orcs the moment their back's turned.

Solution: Well, I had to let her go. She took it badly, of course, and actually took me to court[140] for constructive dismissal. The magistrate referred back to my original ad, and determined that not only had she misrepresented herself as an Aussie to get the job, but that she was also both a chancer and, by dint of bringing the court case in the first place, a timewaster, and I had taken the precaution of specifically excluding them from consideration. He satisfied himself in one (short) visit that the pub was indeed exactly as described, and so had no option but to find in my favour. The system works.

Prescription:

   Signed _____

138 My aching bollocks...
139 Of publicans.
140 The Very Small Claims Court, behind the new Asda.

Breathing Exercises

Sometimes your so-called Help Yourself to Wellness expert will try and teach you how to do something bleeding obvious that you know how to do already, like breathing. I've got through life perfectly well with a straightforward IN-OUT approach, but apparently there are more options available, like the following:

INCLUDING the heavy smoker

"IN-IN-IN IN-IN-IN-IN IN-IN-IN"

HAVE YOU tried breathing

(A) THE TRIPLE

In-in-in out-out-out in-in-in
out-out-out (etc)

(B) THE HYPERVENTILATOR

In-in-in-in-in-in-in... Burst! (not advised)

(C) THE PREGNANT LADY

I-i-i-i-n-outoutout....I-i-i-i-i-n-outoutout.
... I-i-i-i-i-n-outoutout....Curse father of
child, vow to make him pay, forswear
sex forever.... And... I-i-i-i-i-n-
outoutout .... (etc)

(D) THE MARATHON RUNNER

In-out in-out in-out in-out in-out in-out in-out (stop at side of road for emergency dump) in-out in-out in-out in-out in-out (feel the burn, push through the burn) in-out in-out in-out in-out (etc)

(E) THE HEAVY SMOKER

In cough up phlegm out, in cough up phlegm out, in cough up phlegm out, in wheeze out, in wheeze out, in cough up phlegm out, in-out, in-out, in-out, gasp, in-out, light up fag, in cough up phlegm out... (etc)

(F) THE POINTLESS BREATH HOLDING EXERCISE

In-in-in hold-hold-hold-hold-hold... Hold... And... Pass out (involuntary) out (involuntary – repeat until consciousness returns) in-out gasp in-out in-out pant in-out. Feel a bit better in-out in-out get a bit cross with breathing exercise in-out in-out breathe more heavily in-out in-out in-out punch wellness expert on nose (repeat until his consciousness fades)

CONCLUSION: Timewasters.

10 Help Yourself to a Better Death

"Who wants to live forever?" asked Freddie Mercury in the Queen song of the same name[141]. Truth is all of us do but none of us will.

Though I have to say I wouldn't like to, being properly in debt[142] can make you seriously grateful that at some point the Grim Reaper might show up and relieve you of your misery, and it wouldn't be much fun being chased around by bailiffs for eternity. How many times could you give them your telly and your sofa before they gave up?

Death is your big (and strictly speaking only) chance to leave a Legacy. A thing by which you shall be remembered. A body of work, perhaps (tricky that one). A reputation (even trickier). As someone who has died in four

separate pub fires[143] and seen four eulogies about myself (I was only driven to heckle once) I am an expert on how to get your Legacy right. Legacies are tricky things too, if you give to charity and don't tell anyone it won't come up at your funeral and people will doubtless think you were a tight selfish

Fig. 1. Closing time (for you)

bastard; give to charity while you're alive and tell people and they'll go on about what a show-off flash do-gooding bastard you are. And having been to my four funerals I can safely say that being slagged off at your funeral (even though strictly speaking you shouldn't be there, you wouldn't hear it and it couldn't possibly matter) is far worse than being slagged off when you're alive. You can't walk up to the bloke and smack him without blowing your cover and ruining the whole thing.

....

[141] "Who Wants To Live Forever".
[142] Of the "are you sure you should be lending me this money?" kind. Let's face it, there are times in everyone's life when if someone's prepared to lend you money they must be more stupid than you are wanting to borrow it.
[143] See *Help Yourself to Deal With Debt*

Grisly Death sequence!!!

★★★★☆   1,588 viewings

Fig. 2. A load of bull

Lots of people are frightened of dying, but one way of looking at it is this: it doesn't matter how you go, you're not going to remember it, are you? Being trampled by a herd of bison charging up the high street would be ghastly (though in Spain some kind of sporting occasion), but if they kill you in the process you won't have to then remember it, or go through repeated trauma and stress and the indignity of having to watch it on YouTube. Your coffin doesn't come with broadband (at least not yet[144]). So in that respect death has a definite upside.

In all things in life, how you exit is easily as important as the entrance you make. As it is we have no say in our entrance into the world, and all of them are pretty similar – back of a cab, maternity ward, pool table in snug potting the black too soon (a loser from day one, my mum used to say), whatever the circumstances, the essentials remain the same, and out of your hands. Death, though, is another matter. As death is the only way out, and in itself offers little dignity, you really need to make sure you've got the exit under control.

....

[144] Trials start 2011

Most people would agree that dying in your bed with all your family around you would be the best way to go, but I haven't seen my boy for eight years so thanks for bringing that up. Though it has to be said it might be good to go out with the wife there and somehow manage to have the last word as I gasped my ultimate – "It was all your fault you stupid cow", something like that, something pithy. Or better still: "You never realised I was rich, did you? I hid all the money under the... aaaaargh..." Then I could go happily to my last rest knowing that she'd be tearing the place apart in a futile quest for her one true love. Loot. Ha ha ha!

There's dying in your sleep, but the problem for me would be getting some, really. I've tried everything you know, everything, but it just won't come. Everything. Booze, no booze, some booze, a little booze, lots of booze suddenly, a bath of booze, warm booze, a light meal, a heavy meal, no meal, sleeping the other way round, going to bed early, not going to bed till I really need to, you name it – it doesn't work. You lie there thinking: "Jesus Christ, when will I ever sleep?!" and your skin is creeping, your scalp itches, your mind is racing and you start to see bugs crawling up the walls (though actually there really are bugs, cockroaches I think, really should do something about that nest in the kitchen; they come through the hole the deep fat fryer blew in the wall). On top of that if you then start thinking about dying in your sleep it's just never going to happen, is it? So I guess I won't be dying in my sleep.

While we're talking about dying in bed, however, what about the prospect of kicking the bucket whilst on the job? That would be fantastic, and to be honest the pursuit of

Fig. 3. Where's my medication?

Fig. 4. It's going to get kicked sooner or later

getting any is killing me anyway. Firstly you need to become a millionaire, I don't know how you're going do this (this is a Help Yourself[145] manual, not the Bumper Book of Bloody Miracles.) Next you need to reach at least eighty years old and make sure you've not looked after yourself one iota throughout your entire life, you know, booze, cigars, the lot. Use your wealth to marry someone at least sixty years your junior, and then just sit back and look forward to that wedding night, because it will be your last on this mortal coil. Wow, what a way to go.

Or, if you're a fan of Elvis, why not cark it on the crapper while eating a burger? Poor old Freddie Mercury died of a cold, which is a bit harder to copy, but the music is his Legacy. You could be found reading a magazine or an improving book perhaps. Then people could unexpectedly have a better opinion of you, such as: "Oh, I didn't know he could read…"

Fig. 5. Made in Heaven (apparently).

Snuffed out unexpectedly has a fair bit going for it. You don't have to waste any time on the planning, for one thing. One minute you're on your way to the Cash 'n' Carry to buy dog food and crisps, the next you've been flattened by the 11.15 to Birmingham New Street. The sort of thing where people afterwards would say: "At least it was quick, he didn't suffer." Apart, of course, from when the bloody train hit me. The trouble is, you have to have sorted your Legacy out, that's the point, because you could be snuffed

[145] £16,000 – interest on a mortgage he had already paid off, **Elliot Morley MP (Lab)**

out unexpectedly at any time (and that's not going to help with the sleeping, either, is it...?)

If you want to be snuffed out unexpectedly and sort your Legacy out at the same time, the thing to do is get yourself assassinated. What you need is to decide on a political stance of some sort (I didn't say it was going to be easy) that is definitely going to upset

some nutters. I can't point out who these are as I don't want to get assassinated myself before I finish the book. Use your imagination. Go on about your stance loads on telly and in the newspapers until you rile the nutters up to fever pitch, and then tell everyone where you are going to be driving around in an open-topped car totally

Fig. 6. What a way to go, eh? Look, I'm even smiling.

unprotected (apart from a couple of bodyguards and what are they going to do exactly, catch the bullet? Me neither, no matter what the perks were of that job). In fact, if you drive around slowly enough blocking all the roads and causing severe gridlock, eventually someone late for an appointment at the clap clinic will lose their marbles stuck in the traffic jam you've caused with your bloody motorcade and shoot you. Hey presto, you're dead, you've been assassinated, and by a bloke who pisses razorblades. What a Legacy. How important you must have been. And also you've proved to the Austrians it can be done without causing a World War. What's more you will have groups of devoted people dedicating their whole lives to proving that the person who clearly did shoot you didn't actually shoot you and that it was the CIA bloke driving your car from behind a grassy knoll, whatever they are.

Dying an heroic death looks like a good option. Going back into a burning building is an extremely brave thing to do, trust me, and certainly isn't something you ever get used to. The second and third times I'd left Ramrod in the snug – the first time he came running out after me.

Fig. 7. Blue Cross Sale

The good thing about dying an heroic death is that your death is your Legacy, they're one and the same. Your heroic death is the only thing people remember about you when you've gone. Storming a machine gun nest, dagger between your teeth, falling on a grenade to save your comrades – if that's how people remember you you'll always be thought of as a great bloke, no matter how much porn you watched or how much money you owed. OK, there might not be enough of you left to pin the medal to, but the thing is you'll have a Legacy. Worth thinking about.

In many ways dying is like Saturday night: the most important thing is to make sure you don't go out looking stupid, or just faintly pointless. I'm not saying leave an attractive corpse, necessarily, just make sure the main talking point at your funeral is not how you fell out of a tree in your underpants or something.

Fig. 8. Ready for work

Fig. 9. Nice vest

And if you can combine all of the above into a kind of Super Death –
let's say you're on the toilet, eating a burger, shagging a bird, with all your
family watching you fall asleep, and you get taken out by a sniper, thus
saving someone's life, and it all happens really unexpectedly – well, then
you're dying the dream, aren't you?

Fig. 10. Supersize me

10.1 Famous Last Words

An important ingredient of Helping Yourself to a Better Death is the business of your Famous Last Words. If the last thing you say is somehow witty or telling, again, your Legacy will receive a (probably) much-needed boost. And final words can also offer a simple snapshot of the person exiting this world and entering "a different sphere of consciousness", as the weird midget lady with the big glasses in *Poltergeist* called it. Oscar Wilde went out saying: "Either that wallpaper goes, or I do", which just proves, yet again, that he was of the gay-fella/bloke persuasion, and even as the Light hoved into view ("stay away from the Light, Carol-Anne" *ibid.*) all he really cared about was interior decoration. Laurence Llewelyn-Bowen will doubtless be saying something similar as he exits, but at least he occupies the unique position of being The Exception That Proves The Rule.

Here's seven Famous Last Words that you will have heard before doubtless but which have become the gold standard words of departure, and my Helpful interpretation of what they mean

i. Julius Caesar went for: "Et tu, Brute" *trans* "And you Brutus". Caesar said this while being stabbed in the back by loads of his mates – and leading them was his best pal Brutus. Even in death Caesar stuck firmly

ONE MORE FOR THE ROAD, BRUTUS?

Fig. 11. That's a good head, Julius

to the ancient and noble business of making sure everyone got their round in. Poetry that is, and it doesn't even rhyme.

ii. **Winston Churchill**, world's greatest man and king of sayings, said: "I'm bored with it all". Well, if he was bored there's no hope for any of us, is there? And if he'd just hung around for another three years he'd have been in time for the advent of colour television. What that tells us though is that he had extremely high standards, if you're bored after defeating Hitler and Saving The World From Evil, you're never going to be satisfied, are you?

iii. **Noel Coward** brought down the final curtain with: "Goodnight my darlings, I'll see you tomorrow". No, you won't, Noel. Let himself down there really. And he was supposed to be good with words, too.

iv. **Henry VIII** bowed out with: "All is lost! Monks, monks, monks!". That tells you that a man can have six wives and still be concerned with something, anything else[146].

v. **Dylan Thomas,** writer and layabout[147] said: "I've had eighteen straight whiskies, I think that's the record…". This just shows how out of touch writers are, everyone knows that the *Guinness Book of Records* doesn't accept gluttony

Stitch that, Hitle

[146] These last words were later covered by the band Sailor in their hit "Girls Girls Girls". By the seventies people were more interested in girls than monks.
[147] As if there's any other kind.

records anymore, and it certainly doesn't count if it kills you.

vi. When asked if dying was tough the actor **Edmund Gwenn** said: "Yes, it's tough, but not as tough as doing comedy". Well, you've either got it or you ain't mate.

vii. "Kiss me Hardy!" croaked **Admiral The Lord Admiral Lord Horatio Nelson**, according to legend, though it is well documented that he actually said: "Thank God I have done my duty… Drink drink, fan fan, rub rub…" while Hardy tapped the side of his head and looked concerned for his sanity.

10.2 Timing!

The trouble is if you've thought of a good one you HAVE TO GET YOUR TIMING RIGHT. The French author Victor Hugo's Famous Last Words were: "I see black light"[148]. Now there's no doubt that he had that one ready, it's a cracker, it sounds poetic, it hints at what's to come, it makes him sound like he's got a proper imagination on him and an excellent command of the language (even if it was originally in French) – it's a corker.

....

[148] You're right, there's no way I should know about a French author (though he may have written the book that summed up the French – at least judging by the title – *Les Miserables*) but for this one I resorted to the interweb.

Fig. 12. Death bed scene

But the real problem is making sure that you really are about to die when you utter your killer (for want of a better word) expression. There is no point polishing up a brilliant set of Famous Last Words and saying them half an hour too early. What if the nurse comes back in and offers you another cuppa? You'd have to keep schtum even though you're really thirsty. As if dying wasn't bad enough as it is without gasping as well.

So, to make sure your exit is all taken care of, once you've uttered the words that history will forever remember, you have to sign the do-not-resuscitate form, lie back and wait for the inevitable. You can't say, "actually I need to go for a pee" or "what time is it?" or "can we switch that over to *Eastenders*?" because you'll blow the whole thing. Worst case scenario is, of course, if your condition starts to improve and you get better, because then you're going to have to come up with a whole new set of Famous Last Words. The last thing you want to do is say them again and have your mates all go: "Heard it!".

There's also the business of making sure that someone has a pen and paper to hand, and that you say the Famous Last Words loud and clear so that they get heard properly. You don't want to say something cool and nonchalant like: "Life is a roll of the dice..." only to have someone write down that your last words were: "My wife gets a Rolls Royce". Of course, if you've got the strength to say things loud and clear and the wit to say something good, it does rather call into question whether you shouldn't be using this last ounce of strength to fight off your impending, but trust me, getting these words right is essential, if only because they can be used to distract attention away from all sorts of stuff.

Once you've made sure you've shuffled off this mortal quietly and soberly (though I'm not saying you have to be sober, in fact quite the opposite), then you need to make sure you have sorted a top flight funeral. Not in that order, obviously. It's crucial to get this right. Your family and friends are going to forget what you were like soon enough, and what you want them to remember of you, if you can make it happen, is the best send off imaginable.

Fig. 13. Make the final journey in style

10.3 Your Funeral

When Lady Di[149] died the whole nation mourned and if you didn't there was something wrong with you, frankly.

Tears and flowers and tears, and lots of people drinking away the grief. Happy days. It's never that busy in September round the back-to-school time. Jackpot. But it has to be said that while her funeral was the best funeral there has ever been, right down to her brother having the sheer brass neck to go on about Family in front of the world (you have to love the posh, they just carry on as though no one has noticed any of it) some people really didn't know how to behave. I'm talking about the moment when her coffin emerged from wherever they were keeping it, and people clapped. Let's just get one thing straight: clapping at a funeral is a Bad Thing, you do not clap at funerals.

Your own funeral has got to be a bit special. It doesn't have to a be a horse-and-carriage whole-East-End-grinds-to-a-halt-to-pay-warped-respects-Kray-type funeral, but it does have to be a decent

[149] She was a Candle In The Wind. "Di Dead Dodi Dead" – I'll never forget that headline.

send-off. Having been to four of my own funerals I think I can safely say I am an expert. So to make your funeral special you need to make preparations. You obviously want your name spelt out in flowers along the coffin, that always looks great. Mine would say GUV, of course, or DAD, if only I'd seen my son in eight years, thanks for bringing that up. For the price of one extra floral letter I could have DEAD, which is not only how I'll be then but how I feel inside now. You might want some kind of special send-off – at my second funeral three of my mates from Landlord Academy did a sawn-off shotgun salute – the full six barrels – but all that did was land them in trouble with Plod on firearms charges, and they did accidentally bring down a heron, so check your local bye-laws first.

Also worth bearing in mind is whether you're going to be buried or cremated. When choosing don't be put off by what these might be like if you were alive. That's just stupid. Grow up. Being cremated offers you the whole-sitting-on-the-mantelpiece-watching-everyone option, as well as the chance to be put into a pair of maracas or something as a bizarre practical joke. The problem with being cremated is that some bright spark will come up with the idea of scattering you in somewhere they think is going to be poignant. All you end up with when this happens is a load of grieving relatives stood on a windy cliff top with a load of furnace-scorched next of kin sticking to the tears on their face and the back of their throats. Disgusting.

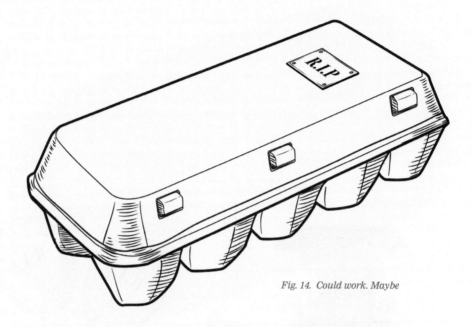

Fig. 14. Could work. Maybe

However, being buried means you get to appoint pall bearers, though that means you need to know some hale and hearty people who are up to the effort of lugging you round. Or else nominate someone you've got a grudge against who might have a dodgy ticker, then you can get the two for one discount. You do run the small risk of being dug up by the animal rights nutters though, which may be a little undignified. And then there's the coffin itself, which, if you ask me is a total waste of wood, that could be put to much better use made into pub bar tops. You're much better going for one of those recyclable things like a giant egg box as it's cheaper, which means more money for the wake so everyone remembers you as a good bloke. Even if you were a tight bastard your whole life, if you chuck in free drinks at your death do then there's no way the guests can slag you off.

Then, of course, you've got the gravestone and most importantly the epitaph to consider. This is a big thing, people will be reading this for years to come so it's got to be clever and pithy, like your Famous Last Words. I'm thinking something that sums up the whole of Man's puny existence on this tiny twinkling planet of ours, something like: 'Boy, Man, Corpse'. Or else: 'Finally, a decent bit of shut-eye.' The trouble is there's no point trying to have anything too clever because as always Churchill's done better than anyone and so don't bother trying to top:

"I AM READY TO MEET MY MAKER. WHETHER MY MAKER IS PREPARED FOR THE GREAT ORDEAL OF MEETING ME IS ANOTHER MATTER"

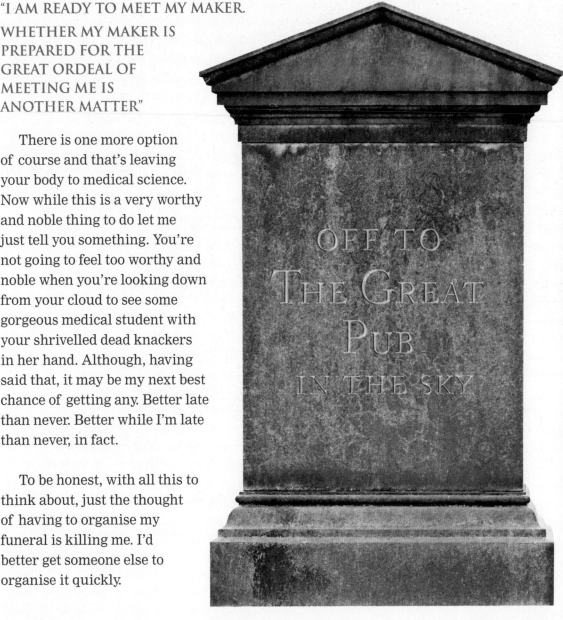

There is one more option of course and that's leaving your body to medical science. Now while this is a very worthy and noble thing to do let me just tell you something. You're not going to feel too worthy and noble when you're looking down from your cloud to see some gorgeous medical student with your shrivelled dead knackers in her hand. Although, having said that, it may be my next best chance of getting any. Better late than never. Better while I'm late than never, in fact.

To be honest, with all this to think about, just the thought of having to organise my funeral is killing me. I'd better get someone else to organise it quickly.

10.4 What Next Then?

So, you're dead and dignified, your funeral went off perfectly and without a hitch, now what?

You will probably have your own views on what comes next. The eternal echoing black void of nothingness is the most likely in my opinion. You know, same old same old.

You could subscribe to the idea that there is an eternity of paradise, with clouds and harps and so on, but that doesn't seem like much to look forward to, to me. I mean, why wouldn't you just keep falling right through the clouds? That would keep me awake at nights, and I've had enough of that in this life, frankly.

Still, you'd get to listen to the band that God has been putting together, you know the one. Freddie on vocals, Elvis and Lennon on backing, Keith Moon on drums, Hendrix and Harrison on guitars, Beethoven on keyboards, with Buddy Holly, the Big Bopper, Sinatra, Cobain and Morrison on the sub's bench – although that must be frustrating for them, because when are they ever going to get on stage? What can go wrong? They're in Heaven. And by the way when is Le Bon going to get the call up?

10.5 *What else is there?*

What about reincarnation? The dangers are obvious: there's always the risk that if you come back as a woman you end up liking going to bed with fellas. I will never be confused, not in this life or any other.

It has been argued (in the snug bar last August as it happens) that for anyone's money the ways animals behave pretty much tells you that they are people who've been reincarnated. You'll notice flies are awfully quiet when they eat; they're full of disgust, as would you be if faced with a plate of shit for dinner; after all this is why they don't live that long – they're trying to die and come back as something else. I, for one – though I reckon as ever I speak for many – could never really put my back into being a fly.

But if you want to take seriously the idea of Helping Yourself to a good next life, you need to watch how you behave in this life. The big idea is what you come back as is either a punishment or a reward for the way you have occupied your time this time on the planet. This needs to be taken seriously, especially when you consider how it is that lobsters die in restaurants.

Lobsters die horribly in restaurants, in one of two ways. Either a giant knife is plunged through the cranium – there's a cross like mark on the top of the head that helpfully offers somewhere to aim at, and then the middle tail flap is grabbed, twisted and pulled out, removing the "poo pipe" as its known, or "shit tube" for the less coy. The other way of killing a lobster is – with a tea towel

PRINCESS MARGARET   **MOTHER TERESA**

to protect you from the barbs on its exo-skellington – to grab the tail, twist it off, then pull off the claws, and simply leave the head end to sit there watching the ~~chef~~ cook tear out the poo pipe. That would be no way to go whatsoever. So next time you're about to cut someone up at a roundabout, touch up your brother's wife, get a job in my brother's wine bar (the Judas), or not get your round in (I don't care if you're broke), think of how you might one day watch a man in cook's whites tear out your backside while the darkness (and boiling water) closes in around you.

On the bright side, it's also fun considering who you'd like to come back as a lobster. In fact, it always passes a jolly hour or two in the pub. My top candidate is usually that builder from the North who ripped me off four years ago, only on condition that I'm the ~~chef~~ cook who gets to dismember him and then he comes back as a lobster again and I get to do it again. And again. (You see, I haven't forgotten, you know who you are and I know where you live...) Then there's Diego Maradona, of course – let him see how easy it is to use the Hand of God when it's delicately broiling on the other side of the kitchen to his arse. Alan (you know, Steve, Steve and Steve's mate) always suggests anyone who eats lobster, because it's poncy food, and he likes the idea that when their claws were torn off it would be with an ironical twist.

Anyway, that's the afterlife for you. Take your pick.

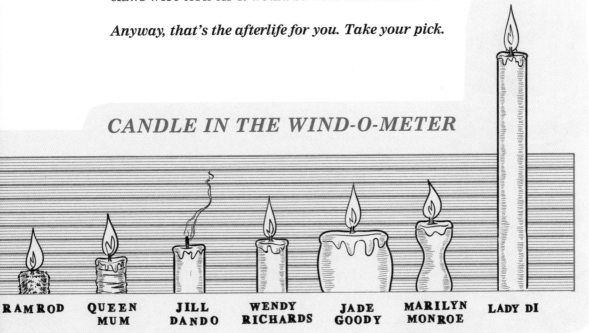

CANDLE IN THE WIND-O-METER

RAMROD QUEEN MUM JILL DANDO WENDY RICHARDS JADE GOODY MARILYN MONROE LADY DI

Conclusion

So, you've read this far, and you've taken on board what I've said. Your life is no longer stuck on the mini roundabout of indecision, you've now selected your exit, indicated, and you're gunning the gas for the right turning (not the left turning, you must get that by now, though when you think about it when you're on a roundabout all the turnings are left even if you're turning right, I haven't thought this through and it's in the conclusion, sod it, it'll do).

So what have we learnt? That low expectations lead to success. That doctors are on the make. That eggs make you constipated. This and much else. Check the index for more, or buy another copy and start again at the beginning, if only there was a way for this book to destroy itself like in *Mission: Impossible* before you'd memorised its contents, I'd be minted.

Having said all that, this book does not contain all the answers. Of course not, that would be ridiculous, and for two reasons. First of all I don't have all the answers for you in particular (though I admit I did say that I did have all the answers at the start of this book) because I haven't a clue what your actual problems are. And secondly, if I gave all the answers away there'd be no book for you to buy once you've read this one. Because the whole thing about me Help You to **Helping Yourself** is You have Helped me to **Help Myself**. Good luck Tommy!

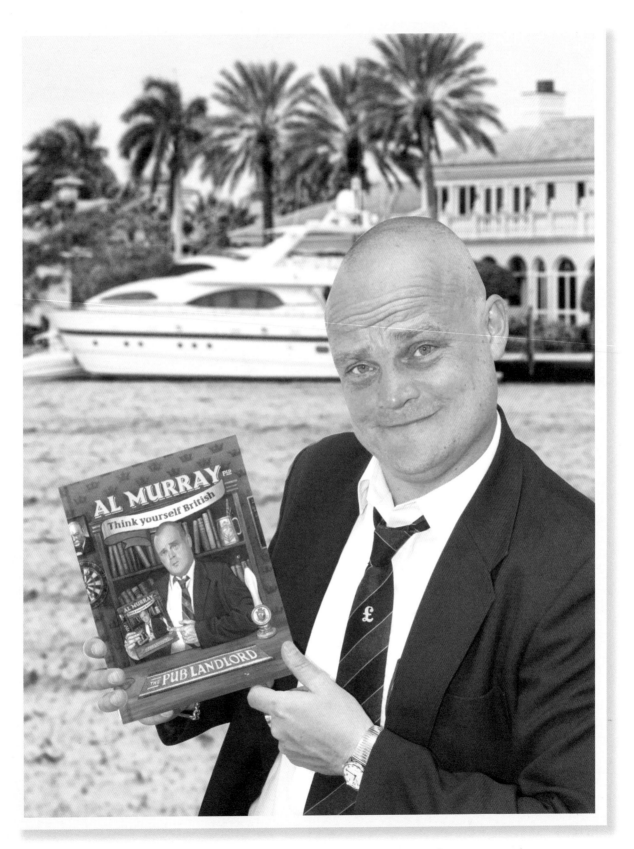

Helping You to Help Myself...

Like to play golf, but find it hard to keep up? Try the Tolliver's revolutionary seven hole golf course. It's eleven holes easier than a conventional course, freeing up eleven holes worth of *BRAIN***SPACE**™!

The Tolliver seven hole golf course.

Our rooms are sparsely furnished but functional, since the question "Why is there hardly any furniture?" takes up far less *BRAIN***SPACE**™ than working out how to make sure the porn channels don't show up on your credit card bill.

*A BRAIN***SPACE**™ *saving bedroom!*

Our fully-equipped restaurant serves one starter (melon boat), one main course (chicken), and one dessert (brown and white ice cream). That means no more time-consuming wrangling with troulesome menus, more *BRAIN***SPACE**™ saved!

It is an established science-esque *FACT* that men think about sex every 15 minutes, wasting valuable *BRAIN***SPACE**™, but not on the *BRAIN***SPACE**™ Think-Away Weekend! We have lumped all those 15-minutely sessions into one Bumper Lap-Dancing Evening! You can think about sex for up to four and a half hours, freeing up the rest of the day's *BRAIN***SPACE**™ for other important thoughts!

ONLY **£1.775.99***
for the complete
*BRAIN***SPACE**™
Think-away
Weekend

*And once you've coughed this up, you'll have more space between your ears than even you realised!

Thinking about it wastes your *BRAIN***SPACE**™

Free your *BRAIN***SPACE**™!

Discover your BRAIN'S PACE™!

Don't just think about it
BOOK IT!!!

Call 020 789 645, ask for Sal.
16 Gillford Road
Dorking SE8 5DW.

Suggested Further Reading:

In the interests of helping you to Help Yourself[150], here are some more books to read that will help to put you on the path to personal wellness. I urge you to get the hardbacks, they last longer, and buy them at the full RRP not knocked down with some sort of cut-price sticker on the front. Feel good about yourself, for Christ's sake. Wellness starts here.

The Pub Landlord's Book of British Common Sense[151] – Al Murray the Pub Landlord, *Hodder and Stoughton* (2007).

Flonsters! – Al Murray the Pub Landlord, *Hodder and Stoughton* (2008).

More Flonsters! – Al Murray the Pub Landlord, *Hodder and Stoughton* (2008).

Flonsters at Sea – Al Murray the Pub Landlord, *Hodder and Stoughton* (2009).

Flonster Wars – Al Murray the Pub Landlord, *Hodder and Stoughton* (2009).

Flonsters V: The Slackening – Al Murray the Pub Landlord, *Hodder and Stoughton* (due 2010).

Flonsters the TV Series Untitled Book Spin-off – Al Murray the Pub Landlord, *TVTimes Publications*[152] (due 2010).

Flonsters: The Merchandising Catalogue – available direct from *www.flonstermuchmoneysendnow.co.uk*[153]

My Miserable Life – Al Murray the Pub Landlord, *Hodder and Stoughton* (2009).

More of my Bloody Miserable Life – Al Murray the Pub Landlord, *Hodder and Stoughton* (due 2010)[154].

The Ramrod Adventures – Al Murray the Pub Landlord, *Hodder and Stoughton* (2009).

Cook Yourself British – Al Murray the Pub Landlord, *Hodder and Stoughton* (2009).

A Brief History of Time Gentlemen Please – Al Murray the Pub Landlord, *Hodder and Stoughton* (2009).

---

[150] £440.62 – chauffeur company bill – **George Osborne MP (Cons)**
[151] Not got one yet? What's wrong with you?
[152] Once they agree to pay through the nose for it.
[153] Or go straight to the website and buy them. We can hardly knock them out fast enough.
[154] Provided enough new miserable things happen to me in the meantime. Otherwise I'll have to start making some up.

Acknowledgements

Cheers doesn't just mean cheers, as in "cheers!". It also means thank you. So, I say "cheers!" (not "cheers!" though) to the following:

Mark Augustyn and Chris "Eggs" England, regular drinkers and British Thinkers, the real Steve, Steve, Alan and Steve, two men doing the work of four.

The Brewery, aka Avalon: Richard Allen Turner, Jon Thoday, James Taylor, Dan Lloyd, Jo Cross.

Adam Booker: designated driver and so much else.

The team at Hodder, bless you, you had me back: Ben, Jack, Jamie, Lucy, Aslan, Leni,and the rest.

Unreal-uk.com – it looks so good you don't even need to read it.
Job's a good'un.

Everyone who bought the last book (*The Book of British Common Sense*) thanks to you this book is happening! Cheers! (not "Cheers!")

Photo Credits

Alamy: 114 (top), 141, 157, 190 (top), 195, 255; Collegedrinker.com: 229; Corbis: 97, 208, 237; CosgroveHall/Everett/Rex Features: 216 (right); © Felix the Cat Productions, Inc: 216 (left); Getty Images: 12 (bottom left), 12 (bottom right), 14, 16, 17, 85, 126 (bottom), 206, 221, 235, 236, 249, 250 (Mercury), 250 (Moon); IndependentMail.com: 244; ITV/Rex Features: 92-93, 121; Roy Kilcullen: 29 (left); Mary Evans: 15; MGM/The Kobal Collection: 243; New Line/The Kobal Collection/Peter Sorel: 78 (centre left); Paramount/Everett/Rex Features: 183; Pyzam.com: 71; Rex Features: 7, 12 (centre right, top left & right); 31, 34, 46, 50, 53, 76, 93, 94, 95 (centre right), 103, 104, 111, 113, 120, 121, 127, 177, 190 (bottom), 196, 201, 204, 205, 207, 209 (right), 213, 234, 239 (top), 241, 245, 249-250 (Jackson, Elvis & Lennon), 252; Universal/Everett/Rex Features: 192; Warner Brothers/ The Kobal Collection: 238 (left). Note: Poindexter is © TM of FTCP,Inc. All rights reserved. All the images of Poindexter and traits, peculiarities, personality and character are unique to Poindexter as are its trademarks and copyrights worldwide. *All other images either Shutterstock or created by the tender loving hands of Unreal Ltd.*

itv DVD

AL MURRAY
THE PUB LANDLORD

BEAUTIFUL BRITISH TOUR LIVE AT

The O2

BRAND NEW DVD
AVAILABLE FROM
NOV 09

"A NATIONAL TREASURE"
★★★★★
DAILY TELEGRAPH

15

15

15

DVD VIDEO

SUMXXXX

Index to **THINK YOURSELF BRITISH**

F

G

H